The
Day Hiker's Guide
to Stanley, Idaho

by Scott Marchant

46 hikes within 30 miles of Stanley, Idaho

Published by
Hiking Idaho
P.O. Box 9498
Boise, ID 83707

Manufactured in the United States

Book Design by Angela R. Stewart Design, Inc.
Cover Photograph: Sawmill Basin by Thad Gerheim

All photographs by the author except as noted

Library of Congress Control Number: 2009927859
Marchant, Scott, 1962-

ISBN-10   0-98247-240-4
ISBN-13   978-0-98247-240-8

Liability Waiver

Due to the possibility of personal error, typographical error, misinterpretation of information, and the many changes both natural and man-made, The Day Hiker's Guide to Stanley, Idaho, its author, publisher, and all other persons or companies directly and indirectly associated with this publication assume no responsibility for accidents, injury, damage or any losses by individuals or groups using this publication.

Outdoor activities are always potentially dangerous. Good decision-making skills and astute judgement will help reduce potential hazards and risks. Prepare yourself with proper equipment and outdoor skills, and you will be able to have an enjoyable experience.

Every effort has been made to assure the accuracy of the information in this book. Corrections and updates are welcome, and may be sent to the author at scottma@mac.com.

HIKES NORTH OF HIGHWAY 21

Bull Trout Lake Area

Bear Valley Area

Langer Lake Area

Lola Creek/Marsh Creek Area

HIKES SOUTH OF HIGHWAY 21

North Sawtooth Area

Stanley Lake Area

Iron Creek Area

HIKES NORTH OF STANLEY ALONG HIGHWAY 75

Sunbeam Area

Casino Creek Area

Lower Stanley Area

HIKES SOUTH OF STANLEY/EAST OF HIGHWAY 75

Boundary Creek Area

Southern White Clouds

HIKES SOUTH OF STANLEY/WEST OF HIGHWAY 75

Alturas Lake Area

Pettit Lake Area

Hell Roaring Creek Area

Redfish Lake Area

Introduction

If a hiker had to pick one area to hike for the remainder of his or her life, Stanley, Idaho would have to get top choice. The small community is surrounded by mountain scenery that rivals Yosemite National Park or Rocky Mountain National Park. Fortunately, the hordes of visitors who visit these National Parks are not to be found.

The Stanley Basin is sheltered by four rugged mountain ranges: the Salmon River Mountains, the Sawtooths, the Boulder Mountains and the White Clouds. The amount of wild geography to play in is mind-boggling. The Sawtooth Mountains and the 217,000-acre Sawtooth Wilderness lie to the southwest of Stanley. The 450,000-acre White Clouds and Boulder Mountains shoulder the east and southeast. Both of these areas are components of the vast, 756,000- acre Sawtooth National Recreation Area.

To the north of Stanley sit the rugged Salmon River Mountains, part of the 2.36 million-acre Frank Church River of No Return Wilderness area and the largest wilderness area in the lower 48 states. It's estimated that the Frank Church alone has 2,700 miles of trails leading off from more than 65 trailheads.

This guide identifies key hikes near Stanley, Idaho and gives you essential and accurate information. The three key parameters in deciding which hikes to include were:

- The trailheads had to be within 30 miles of upper Stanley
- All the trailheads had to be accessible by a passenger car
- The hikes could be no more than 15 miles out and back

This guide includes hikes of varying lengths and difficulty. Many of the hikes include a family-friendly description in the initial section of the hike for those with children who may want a shorter hike. In this description, you will find great places, usually within one to two miles, to turn around, picnic, or just take in the wonderful scenery.

You do not have to embark on a weeklong journey into the backcountry to enjoy this special place. A morning or afternoon hike along a bubbling creek or through a wildflower-filled meadow will reveal this remarkable area. It is hoped that this guide will ultimately provide you with a multitude of everlasting memories.

How To Use This Book

Each hike in this book has four primary sections:

- 11 key, at-a-glance details that can help you choose the ideal hike

- A general overview of the scenery that will be seen on the hike

- Trailhead directions from upper Stanley

- A detailed description of the hike

Throughout the text, you will find cumulative distances so that you can tailor any particular hike to fit your own time constraints or desires.

The at-a-glance details include:

GPS Coordinates - Thanks to current technology, we are in an age of affordable tracking devices courtesy of Global Positioning System (GPS) and wireless communications. Every lake, trailhead, mountain and even person can be positioned, mapped and monitored. Many automobiles, watches, and various handheld devices have the capability to let you know your exact location. This is achieved by many satellites sending signals to receivers, including watches, handheld devices, autos, and other receivers that use the information to calculate exact positions.

The GPS uses the World Geodetic System 1984 datum which is the most widely used and accurate datum today (also known as WGS84). When you buy a GPS unit, this setting is most likely the default when you turn on your GPS for the first time. Most GPS units have the capability to set the datum field. Current or up-to-date United States Geological Survey maps generally use NAD83 (to make things more confusing, this is nearly the same as WGS84). Many older maps use the North American Datum of 1927 (NAD27). The 7.5 quads for most of the hikes in this book are NAD27 because they were last updated in the 1960s and 1970s. The Sawtooth and White Cloud Mountains Trail Map utilizes NAD83. The Earthwalk Press map for the Sawtooth Wilderness does not show GPS coordinates at all.

All GPS coordinates in this book were obtained using a handheld GPS unit withWGS84 datum. If you use a GPS, make sure it is set to navigate with WGS84 data. The coordinates for trailheads and final destinations are provided in degrees, with minutes as decimals.

You don't need a GPS device to use this book. Readers can get to all trailheads and complete the hikes from the hike's description. GPS coordinates are included for those individuals who enjoy GPS technology.

Distance: Distances are given in round-trip mileage and are given to the closest 1/10 of a mile. The distances have been measured from the trailhead to the hike's final destination. All distances were measured with a handheld GPS.

Total elevation gain: This shows how much climbing you will be doing. Because all but one of the hikes are out and back, the total elevation gain is the cumulative amount of climbing required from the trailhead to your final destination and then back to the trailhead. To compute the TOTAL elevation gain for a hike, the elevation gain was added with the elevation loss. For example, on an out and back hike, if you hike up 1,000 feet then descend 400 feet, your total gain for that particular hike is 1,400 feet. That's because on your return, you will need to hike back up the 400 feet you descended.

Difficulty: Each trip is subjectively rated for its difficulty by identifying the trail as easy, moderate, difficult or very difficult. The rating is based on an individual in relatively good physical condition. There is some variation within each category.

Easy - 1 to 6 miles with less than 800 feet of total elevation gain.

Moderate - 5 to 9 miles with less than 1200 feet of total elevation gain.

Difficult - 6 to 12 miles with more than 2000 feet of total elevation gain.

Very Difficult - 10 to 15 miles and more than 2000 feet of elevation gain.

Elevation Range - These figures represent the trail's highest and lowest points, not necessarily the beginning and ending elevations. Normally, the lowest elevation will be the trailhead. Elevations are given in feet and rounded to the nearest 50 feet. For example, if a hike ends at a peak of 9,877 feet, it is listed as 9,900 feet. Use these numbers to analyze how high a particular hike travels. This information is valuable if you are vulnerable to altitude sickness. Or if you are hiking in early season, you can predict whether you might encounter snowfields. The Forest Service can give you an estimate for the elevation you might find snow, in early season hiking.

Topographic Map or Topo: This refers to the United States Geological Survey (USGS) maps that cover a particular hike. These maps are the most detailed available and show nearly every road, track, trail, water body and vegetation. They are on a 1:24,000-scale topographic maps, also known as 7.5'-minute quadrangles. This type of scale is known as a ratio scale; one inch is equal to 24,000 inches (or 2,000 feet) in the real world. Another way to look at it is that objects on the map have been reduced 1/24,000 of their original size.

The downside to the 7.5' quad is that many of the USGS topos are outdated because they were created 30 to 40 years ago. Although the mountains and lakes have not changed, roads and trails may have. If a hike is not indicated or has been relocated on a particular quad, it is noted in the text.

One final feature of the 7.5' quads is contours. Topographic contours are shown by lines of different widths. Each contour line is a line of equal elevation; therefore, contours never cross. The 7.5' quads show the contour interval at 40 feet. Contours that are very close together represent steep slopes. Widely spaced contours or an absence of contours means that the ground slope is relatively flat.

The 7.5' quads can be purchased in Stanley at the Stanley Ranger Station just south of town on Highway 75. They carry various USGS 7.5' quads for the Sawtooth National Recreation Area, but not the Salmon-Challis National Forest or quads north of Highway 21. You can also get USGS 7.5 quads, including many from the Salmon-Challis National Forest and the Boise National Forest, at McCoy's Fish and Tackle in downtown Stanley. Other sources for the USGS 7.5' quads in Idaho include most outdoor gear stores in Boise, Ketchum, and Twin Falls. Finally, if you have the time, you can order maps directly from the U. S. Geological Survey at www.usgs.gov/pubprod/.

It is not necessary to have the USGS 7.5' maps to complete any hike in this book. But the 7.5' quads are the way to go if you want to see yourself hike along the trail across the map.

Estimated Time: It is impossible to accurately predict your hiking time because everybody hikes at a different speed. It is generally accepted in the hiking world that the average day hiker will fall between 2 to 3 miles per hour on a relatively level trail. If you are backpacking your pace will be much slower because of the extra weight. If a trail has elevation gain — and most of these do—the speed drops in direct proportion to the trail's steepness.

Time is listed in two ranges. The first time listed is for a fast hiker averaging 3 miles per hour on level ground. To account for elevation gain, 30 minutes is added to the time for every 1,000 feet of gain. The second time listed is for a slow hiker averaging 2 miles per hour on level ground. To account for elevation gain, 45 minutes is added to the time for every 1,000 feet of gain. Most hikers will fall somewhere in between the two figures. The times listed are for hiking only. They do not include lunch, snacks, photography, or off-trail explorations. Many factors can slow you down such as wet trails, poor weather visibility, snow, difficult stream crossings, and altitude acclimation.

Distance to Trailhead: This is the distance from the intersection of Highway 21 and Highway 75 in Stanley to the trailhead.

Water Availability: Where you can reliably find water. Creeks, lakes and side streams are indicated. All sources listed are reliable throughout the summer.

Cautionary Advice: *This will alert you to possible hazards on a particular hike. Just because a hike is easy or moderate does not mean it does not have hazards. For instance, the hike to Bridal Veil Falls is listed as moderate if based on distance and elevation gain but about halfway into the hike, a difficult stream crossing may be impossible to cross in early season. You will have to use your own good judgement. This creek crossing will be noted in the cautionary advice section.*

For Additional Information: This section gives the appropriate forest agency and district phone number for the area where the trail is located.

Leave No Trace Principles

It is important to respect the wilderness so all visitors can enjoy the experience. The trails in this book travel through beautiful, yet fragile, country. Take time to learn Leave No Trace ethics and apply these principles to the outdoors. Please teach your children these manners because they will soon be the stewards of this wonderful expanse of country.

Plan Ahead and Prepare

- Take the time to know the regulations.
- Prepare for extreme weather conditions, emergencies, and unexpected hazards.
- Keep your group size to parties of 6 or fewer.
- Let someone know where you will be hiking and when you plan on returning.

Respect Wildlife

- Observe wildlife from a distance and do not approach.
- Never feed wildlife.
- Have pets under control at all times.

Leave the Land As You Found It

- Do not pick wildflowers and other plants. Leave it for the next person to enjoy.
- Leave natural objects such as rocks and vegetation as you find them.
- Do not destroy or remove cultural and historic structures and relics.
- If you pack something into the wilderness, PACK IT OUT.

Travel and Camp Impacts

- Do not cut switchbacks. This causes erosion and additional trail maintenance.
- In groups, try to walk single file. The vegetation on the sides of the trail is extremely fragile.
- Select durable surfaces such as rock, gravel, and dry grass for lunch and snack spots.
- Avoid places where you see the beginning signs of human impact.

Dispose of Waste Properly

- Deposit human waste in catholes 6 to 8 inches deep and at least 200 feet from trails and water.
- Cover the catholes with a piece of downed wood.
- Do not leave toilet paper in the wilderness. PACK IT OUT.

Be Considerate of Other Visitors

- Be courteous and yield to other users.
- Yield to horses or pack stock by stepping downhill.
- Respect other visitors. Avoid loud noises.
- Let the quiet and solitude of the wilderness rule.

Regulations

Specific to hikes located in the Sawtooth Wilderness.

Permits

- All wilderness users must have a wilderness permit.
- Self-issued wilderness permits are available at trailheads and certain points along trails when officially entering the wilderness.
- Groups larger than 8 or more people must obtain a permit from a Forest Service Office.
- Groups may not exceed 12 people May 1 to November 30.

Dogs

- Dogs must be on leash on trails from July 1 to Labor Day.

Fire

- Campfire restrictions exist and some areas are closed to campfires. Check with the Sawtooth National Recreation Area, Stanley Ranger Station (208) 774-3000.

Hiking Safety

Lightning - In 2007, it was reported that 45 people in the United States were killed by lightning. Four of the 45 were hikers. In the summer, mountain thunderstorms typically form during the early afternoon. Storms can build quickly and hikers should be constantly observing weather conditions. If lightning threatens, get below the treeline. Keep out of meadows and away from lone trees or rocks. If you are caught in an exposed location, discard metal objects and squat on two feet, keeping as low to the ground as possible. Also, stay at least 20 feet away from others in your group so that one strike does not incapacitate your entire hiking group.

Hypothermia - Hypothermia in simple terms, occurs when more heat escapes from your body than your body can produce. Initial symptoms include possible loss of physical and mental abilities. Severe hypothermia can lead to death.

Hikers tend to overstate the danger of mountain lion and bear attacks. The reality is hypothermia is the more likely killer –up to 700 people a year. All it takes is a few hours in wet, windy weather without proper clothing. Hypothermia can kill in temperatures as high as 50 degrees Fahrenheit.

To help prevent hypothermia, wear proper clothing in layers and take them off or put them on with the changes in your body temperature. Wool and polypropylene clothing are best. Cotton is a bad choice because when it gets wet it can increase conductive heat loss by a factor of five. Always carry good rain gear and wear it when rain threatens.

Heatstroke/Heat Exhaustion - Heatstroke occurs when your body temperature reaches 104 Fahrenheit or higher. It is usually brought on by strenuous physical activity and high environmental temperatures. Heat exhaustion is a milder heat-related syndrome that may include heavy sweating and a rapid pulse. Left untreated, heat exhaustion can lead to heatstroke, a life-threatening condition.

Fortunately, both heatstroke and heat exhaustion are preventable. Drink plenty of liquids and wear a hat. Avoid exposed trails during early afternoon, which can be the hottest part of the day. If someone in your party develops symptoms of heat exhaustion, have the person sit in a shaded or cool place and have them drink plenty of fluids.

Most children cannot be depended on to drink as much water as needed on a hot day. It is the parent's responsibility to ensure the child stays properly hydrated. In the heat of the day, have them drink water every 15 minutes. One idea, to have a little fun, is to announce that it is time for a "WAM," or Water Appreciation Moment.

Creek/Stream Crossings - Water mishaps rank second among outdoor deaths. Use good judgement and don't underestimate creek crossings. When snow melts, creeks, streams, and rivers can rise dramatically, creating a potentially life-threatening situation. As a rule, don't cross fast-moving water that is more than knee deep. When hiking with children, be very careful around high creeks.

Potentially dangerous stream crossings are noted in the trip descriptions. Generally speaking, creek flows are highest in late May and June. Every year is different and depends on the preceding winter's snowfall and the outside temperatures.

Here is some advice for safely fording streams and creeks:

- *Study upstream and downstream and look for a place where the creek is widest.*

- *Make sure your camera, matches, and other items that you would not want to get wet are in watertight containers before you cross.*

- *Walk slowly across the stream and firmly plant each foot before lifting the other foot.*

- *Consider keeping your boots on to help support your ankles and assist in firm footing.*

- *Investigate any downed trees that bridge the creek before you cross. These trees can be very slippery.*

- *Bring a pair of sandals or extra set of shoes to keep your feet dry.*

Altitude Sickness/Acute Mountain Sickness (AMS) - Altitude sickness is a condition caused by exposure to low air pressure, usually outdoors at high altitudes. Symptoms include: headache, vomiting, fatigue, light-headedness and shortness of breath. Altitude sickness can progress to more serious conditions such as high altitude pulmonary edema (HAPE) or high altitude cerebral edema (HACE) that can prove fatal. Both of these conditions do not generally occur until at least 9,000 feet in elevation.

Different people have different susceptibilities to altitude sickness. Some people can show symptoms at 6,500 feet, but most people can hike up to 8,000 feet without problems. To help prevent altitude sickness, do not drink alcohol at high elevations and acclimate your body for 24 hours before ascending above 8,000 feet. The city of Stanley is at an elevation of 6,200 feet, so staying in town for a day before hiking will help with acclimatization.

If symptoms of altitude sickness show up, descend to lower altitudes. Symptoms are usually temporary and will go away after acclimatization.

Your Ego - The most common cause for accidents that trigger search-and-rescue operations is an error in judgement. It was reported that in 2007, insufficient experience and errors in judgement played a role in one-third of the 3,593 search-and-rescue operations in the national park system. Please use common sense.

One bad decision about the weather, off-trail excursions, crossing creeks, or reactions to injuries can lead to big trouble. Stay calm when an emergency presents itself and think about your options.

Hiking With Children

At what age is it appropriate for children to hike? That's your decision based on what you think is right for your family.

Babies

Modern baby backpack carriers, built with extra padding and support, enable parents to hike many miles. The new packs have easy adjustment settings and technical features that help protect babies from the elements. Most babies should be at least 6 months old and weigh at least 16 pounds. If unsure about your baby, talk to your pediatrician.

Toddlers

Of all the age groups, toddlers present the most challenges on a hike. Many toddlers will insist on hiking "all by themselves." Kids at this age can be slow and clumsy, trying any adult's patience. They also tend to tire out easily and then want to be carried. This presents another weighty challenge. Most quality baby backpack carriers can carry up to 40 pounds. This may be an option when the "I'm 2 and there is nothing you can do about it" attitude kicks in.

Age 5 and over

Every child is different, but once they reach age 5 most children can hike several miles. Older children tend to be inquisitive about their surroundings and this offers a great opportunity to teach them about the outdoors. In order to make the trail trip enjoyable, make sure you bring plenty of snacks, candy rewards, and flavored energy beverages. To keep the little ones enthusiastic and motivated try getting them to:

- Find and identify wildflowers along the trail.
- Take as many breaks as needed. A good gauge is to take a break every 15 minutes, which may seem like hours to a child.
- Take time to look for and try to identify animal prints on the trail.
- Help children investigate the rocks, pine cones, and bones that you may find along the trail.

The most important thing is to stay positive and be generous with praise. It's more than likely that everyone will have a wonderful experience. Most of the turnaround spots are within the first 3/4 to 2 miles of the trail. The turnaround spots were chosen because of their features that may appeal to children. This includes lakes, meadows, creek banks, or a viewing spot with nice shade or rock features. Not all trails in the book have highlighted turnaround spots because some trails are too steep or do not have a special feature within that first 3/4 to 2 miles of the trail. Fatigue and lack of interest in children rises quickly when a trail is very steep, has long stretches of the same scenery, or keeps the child directly exposed to the sun.

Kid Hikes

Here is a list of short hikes, all mileages listed as roundtrip, that are recommended with small children. Each of these hikes are the beginning portion of one of the longer hikes in the book. Each of these hikes will have the child symbol indicated near the heading of the title. Please read the main write-up to see if the hike is what you are looking for.

Alice Lake 3.8 miles

Alpine Creek 2.0 miles

Alpine Lake 2.4 miles

Bear Valley Hot Springs 2.6 miles

Big Casino Creek 2.6 miles

Boundary Creek 0.8 miles

Cabin Creek Lakes 3.6 miles

Farley Lake 1.8 miles

Elizabeth Lake 2.4 miles

Elk Meadow 1.4 miles

Fishhook Creek 2.0 miles

Hell Roaring Pond 2.6 miles

Lady Face/Bridal Veil Falls 3.4 miles

Lily Lake/Redfish Lake Creek Falls 1.4 miles

Little Casino Creek 1.4 miles

Lola Creek to the Lola Divide 3.4 miles

Marsh Creek 2.4 miles

Marshall Lake 3.0 miles

Marten/Kelly Lakes 2.0 miles

Redfish Inlet to the Garden of Giants 3.0 miles

Yellow Belly Lake 1.8 miles

Glossary

Ascent - to climb upward

Cairn - A mound of rough stones stacked upon one another built as an indicator of trail direction. Cairns are also sometimes used to identify a landmark such as a mountaintop.

Cirque - a half-open steep-sided hollow at the head of a valley or on a mountainside, formed by glacial erosion

Exposed - no protection or shelter from the sun

Ford - a place in a creek or river that is shallow enough to be crossed by walking or wading

Grade - an ascending, descending or level portion of a hiking trail

Knob - a rounded crest that usually has a view

Outcropping - the part of a rock (usually large) that appears above the surface of the ground

Scramble - climbing over rough terrain

Signed junction - an intersection of two or more hiking trails which are identified with a wooden sign, usually indicating the different trail's name

Snag - a dead tree that is still standing

Switchback - A trail that travels diagonally and then turns back on itself in order to gain ground up a steep section of mountain

Talus - a mass of rock debris at the base of a cliff or slope

Traverse - to go across a mountain hillside sloped on one side

Topographic Map - A map that shows the shape of the Earth's surface by contour lines. Contours are imaginary lines that join points of equal elevation on the surface of the land above or below a reference surface, which in this case is mean sea level. The U.S. Geological Survey (USGS) surveyed the lands within North America and created the various topographic maps. For the purpose of this book, topo (abbreviated version of topographic) maps listed for each hike is the USGS quadrangle (quad) maps that have the greatest amount of detail — the 7.5 minute versions. These maps show contour intervals in 40-feet increments and make it easy to measure the height of mountains, lakes and steepness of slopes.

About The Area

The mountains of central Idaho were formed some 25,000 years ago when glaciers receded, advanced, carved, cut, and eroded the Idaho Batholith. The batholith is the enormous mound of granite that became the Sawtooth Mountains, the White Cloud Peaks and the Boulder Mountains.

Today, Stanley is surrounded by millions of acres of national forest. Within the forest are two very special wilderness areas: The Frank Church River of No Return Wilderness and The Sawtooth Wilderness, part of the larger Sawtooth National Recreation Area.

Frank Church River of No Return Wilderness

The 2.36 million acres of Frank Church River of No Return Wilderness is the largest contiguous area of protected wilderness in the lower 48 states. The southern boundary lies just to the north of Stanley, Idaho. The wilderness offers a number of mountain ranges, including the Salmon River Mountains, the Bighorn Crags and the Clearwater Mountains. The rugged and steep canyons of the Main and Middle forks of the Salmon River divide the mountain ranges.

This protected wilderness was created in 1980 as the River of No Return Wilderness Area. The "River of No Return" is the Salmon River. The river earns the title of No Return because the fast and brisk river currents make upstream travel almost impossible.

In 1984, the area was renamed the Frank Church River of No Return Wilderness Area in honor of Frank Church. Frank Church was a U.S. senator from Idaho who served from 1951 to 1981. He was a strong environmental legislator and played a major role in creating the national Wilderness Act and the Wild and Scenic Rivers Act.

The sheer size of this wilderness area provides an excellent habitat for wildlife. Mountain lions, grey wolves, black bears, lynx, coyote, wolverines, and red fox can be found throughout the area. Other animals may include white tail and mule deer, moose, elk, mountain goats, and bighorn sheep.

Sawtooth National Recreation Area

The Sawtooth National Recreation Area (SNRA) is 756,000 acres and was established by Congress in 1972. It was created "...to assure the preservation and protection of the natural, scenic historic, pastoral and fish and wildlife values, and to provide for the enhancement of the recreation values associated therewith..." of the Sawtooth Valley region of Idaho. The Forest Service protects and manages the area.

The SNRA include three mountain ranges: the White Clouds, the Sawtooths, and the Boulders. Portions of the Smoky mountains fall in the SNRA. The SNRA includes the headwaters of four of Idaho's major rivers, the Boise, the Big Wood, the Payette, and the Salmon.

Source: www.wilderness.net/NWPS/documents/publications/PDF/92-400.pdf

The Sawtooth Wilderness

The 217,088-acre Sawtooth Wilderness is located in the SNRA. In 1972, to ensure better protection for the habitat, the area was upgraded from the status of primitive area to Sawtooth Wilderness. Most of the Sawtooth mountain range falls within this area. The Sawtooth Wilderness includes hundreds of high alpine mountain lakes, nearly 50 peaks over 10,000 feet high, and approximately 270 miles of trail originating from over 40 trailheads.

Wilderness Area

What is a wilderness area? And why? The Wilderness Act of 1964 defines wilderness as "a wilderness, in contrast with those areas where man and his own works dominate the landscape, is hereby recognized as an area where the earth and its community of life are untrammeled by man, where man himself is a visitor who does not remain." The Wilderness Act also defines why we have designated wilderness area: "in order to assure that an increasing population, accompanied by expanding settlement and growing mechanization, does not occupy and modify all areas within the United States and its possessions, leaving no lands designated for preservation and protection in their natural condition..."

To identify an area as wilderness is truly a very special designation meriting that visitors make little or no impact on the land. Please review the section "Leave No Trace Principles" in this guide to ensure that your visit maintains the principles and character of the wilderness designation.

Source: http://www.fws.gov/laws/lawsdigest/wildrns.html

Redfish Lake Lodge

Redfish Lake Lodge is the departure site of several hikes in the book. This 16-acre property is actually on U.S. Forest Service ground and operates on a permit administered by the SNRA.

The lodge was built in 1929 and is located on the north shore of Redfish Lake. Redfish Lake takes its name from the bright red Sockeye Salmon that used to return to the lake from the Pacific Ocean in such large quantities that the lake shimmered red in spawning season.

The lodge has accommodations, a full-service restaurant, general store (they do carry some basic outdoor hiking gear), and a marina. The marina has shuttle boats that go from the lodge to the Redfish Inlet Transfer Camp, which is where several of the hikes in this book start. The boat ride is about 4 miles and takes 10 minutes to complete.

Information regarding costs and departure times (as of the end of 2008; all information was expected to remain the same in 2009):

Shuttle service hours:

Memorial Day to Labor Day: 7 A.M. to 8:30 P.M.

After Labor Day: 8 A.M. to 7 P.M.

Departs marina on demand with two or more individuals

Schedule pick-up to return from the inlet back to the marina: 9 A.M., 12 P.M., 3 P.M., 5 P.M., and 7 P.M.

Costs:

Age 6 and older:	Under 6 years of age:	Dogs:
$8.00 one-way	$4.00 one-way	$3.00 one-way
$15.00 roundtrip	$8.00 roundtrip	$6.00 roundtrip

Hiking Recommendations

To assist you in finding your perfect hike, here is a list of best hikes in several preferences. Every hike in this book has a special quality. Even if it is not listed under one of the "best of" categories, that does not mean that the hike is inferior.

Best Aerobic Hikes

Blue Bunch Mountain *2,400 feet of gain in 8.8 miles roundtrip*

Boundary Creek Trail to the Sunny Gulch Trail *2,750 feet of gain in 8.0 miles roundtrip*

Boundary Creek Trail to the Casino Lakes *3,650 feet of gain in 11.4 miles roundtrip*

Horton Peak *2,750 feet of gain in 6.8 miles roundtrip*

Lola Creek to the Lola Divide *2,550 feet of gain in 9.0 miles roundtrip*

Lookout Mountain *2,650 feet of gain in 11.6 miles roundtrip*

Redfish Inlet to the Baron Divide *2,800 feet of gain in 14.2 miles roundtrip*

Ruffneck Peak *2,400 feet of gain in 8.4 miles roundtrip*

Best Wildflower Hikes

Alice Lake

Alpine Lake

Blue Bunch Mountain

Cabin Creek Lakes

Elk Meadow

Fourth of July Lake/Washington Lake

Rough Lake

Best View Hikes

Alpine Lake

Cape Horn Summit to the Lola Divide

Eureka Gulch

Sawtooth Lake to Sawtooth/McGown Divide

Horton Peak

Lookout Mountain

Lola Creek to the Lola Divide

Hell Roaring Lake to View

Nip and Tuck

Redfish Inlet to the Baron Divide

Redfish Inlet to Alpine Lake

Ruffneck Peak

Twin Lakes

Best Solitude Hikes

Blue Bunch Mountain

Cape Horn Summit to the Lola Divide

Collie Lake

Lola Creek to the Lola Divide

West Fork Of Yankee Creek/Lightning Creek

Rough Lake

Ruffneck Lookout

Best Wildlife-Viewing Hikes

Big Casino Creek

Collie Lake

Elk Meadow

Marsh Creek to the Big Hole

Rough Lake

Best Early Season Hikes

Elk Meadow

Fishhook Creek Trail

Hell Roaring Pond

Lily Lake and Redfish Lake Creek Falls

Little Casino Creek

Marsh Creek to the Big Hole

Nip and Tuck

West Fork of Yankee Creek/Lightning Creek

Best Hikes Along Creeks

Alpine Creek

Bear Valley Creek Hot Springs

Cabin Creek Lakes

Little Casino Creek

Marsh Creek to the Big Hole

Marsh Creek/Big Hole/Middle Fork of the Salmon

Trails By Distance (Roundtrip)

1 to 6 miles

Lily Lake and Redfish Lake Creek Falls 1.4 miles

Nip and Tuck 2.0 miles

Hell Roaring Pond 2.6 miles

Redfish Inlet to the Garden of Giants 3.0 miles

Lady Face Falls 4.8 miles

Yellow Belly Lake 4.8 miles

Elk Meadow 5.0 miles

Langer Lake/Island Lake/Ruffneck Lake 5.2 miles

Kirkham Ridge Trail to Gates Creek 5.4 miles

Fourth of July Lake and Washington Lake 5.6 miles

Alpine Lake 5.8 miles

Fishhook Creek Trail 5.8 miles

6 to 10 miles

Alpine Creek 6.2 miles

Goat Falls 6.8 miles

Horton Peak 6.8 miles

Bear Valley Creek Hot Springs 7.0 miles

Cape Horn Summit to the Lola Divide 7.0 miles

Collie Lake 7.0 miles

Upper Finger Lake 7.4 miles

Redfish Inlet to Flatrock Junction 7.4 miles

Cabin Creek Lakes 7.6 miles

Marten Lake 7.8 miles

Redfish Inlet to Bench Lakes to Redfish Trailhead 7.8 miles

Bridal Veil Falls 7.9 miles

Boundary Creek to the Sunny Gulch Trail 8.0 miles

Eureka Gulch 8.0 miles

Ruffneck Peak 8.4 miles

Blue Bunch Mountain 8.8 miles

Marsh Creek to the Big Hole 9.0 miles

Little Casino Creek 9.0 miles

Lola Creek to the Lola Divide 9.0 miles

Kelly Lake 9.2 miles

Farley Lake 9.4 miles

Rough Lake 9.4 miles

Redfish Trailhead to Marshall Lake 9.6 miles

Elk Meadow/Elizabeth Lake 9.8 miles

Hell Roaring Lake 10.0 miles

Redfish Inlet to the Baron Divide 14.2 miles

Marsh Creek/Big Hole/Middle Fork of the Salmon 14.6 miles

Toxaway Lake 14.6 miles

10 to 15 miles

Redfish Inlet to Alpine Lake 11.0 miles

Alice Lake 11.4 miles

Boundary Creek to the Casino Lakes 11.4 miles

Sawtooth Lake to Sawtooth/McGown Divide 11.5 miles

Lookout Mountain 11.6 miles

Big Casino Creek 12.6 miles

West Fork of Yankee Creek/Lightning Creek 13.0 miles

Twin Lakes 13.6 miles

Hell Roaring Lake to View 13.5 miles

*Everybody's sense of beauty is
different from everybody else's*
                    -Andy Warhol

Kirkham Ridge Trail to Gates Creek

Distance: 5.4 miles roundtrip

Total elevation gain: 900 feet

Difficulty: Moderate

Elevation Range: 6750 feet to 7050 feet

Topographic Map: Bull Trout Point

Time: 2 hours 15 minutes to 3 hours 30 minutes

Distance to trailhead: 28.3 miles

Water Availability: Warm Springs Creek, several side streams, Gates Creek

Cautionary Advice: *This hike enters a burn area with no tree cover. Bring sun protection.*

Additional Information: Boise National Forest, Lowman Ranger District (208) 259-3361

Coordinates
Trailhead:

North 44d18.432
West 115d15.842

Bridge over Gates Creek:

North 44d18.679
West 115d18.744

Kirkham Ridge Trail to Gates Creek

This highly recommended trip to Gates Creek offers great diversity. Although the elevation range from the low point to the high point is only 300 feet, the trail has many ups and downs. This creates more elevation gain than the elevation range suggests.

The first mile of hiking is in healthy forest with several lovely meadows. The trail enters a burn area, a surreal-looking landscape of burnt snags and exposed rock. Next, a section with thousands of young lodgepole trees overtakes the barren landscape. The final destination is bridged Gates Creek, which flows through a very beautiful and rugged canyon.

Trailhead Directions

From Stanley, drive 26.0 miles west on Highway 21. Turn right on forest road 100 towards Bull Trout Lake and Campground. Follow the well graded dirt road 1.9 miles and turn right on a smaller dirt road with a small sign for Kirkham Ridge Trail. Follow this road 0.4 miles to the end of the road.

The Hike

Begin hiking in tree cover with large meadows on both sides of the trail. Cross a couple of platform bridges over marshy areas before gaining elevation above Warm Spring Creek at 0.4 miles. Views down to the scenic creek are splendid.

At 0.8 miles, reach a signed junction. Continue straight, or west, along the Kirkham Ridge Trail. The trail breaks out of forest onto a knoll and enters a burn area at 1.1 miles. Although treeless, this area is particularly scenic with expansive views. The trail descends and crosses three separate streams in quick order.

From the last stream crossing, the trail rises again through an area with thousands of young lodgepoles. Here, an unnamed stream flows along the right side of the trail. The trail eventually levels at a little over 7,000 feet and then descends 300 feet down to the bridge crossing of Gates Creek. On the descent, southern views into the rugged canyon into which Gates Creek flows are terrific.

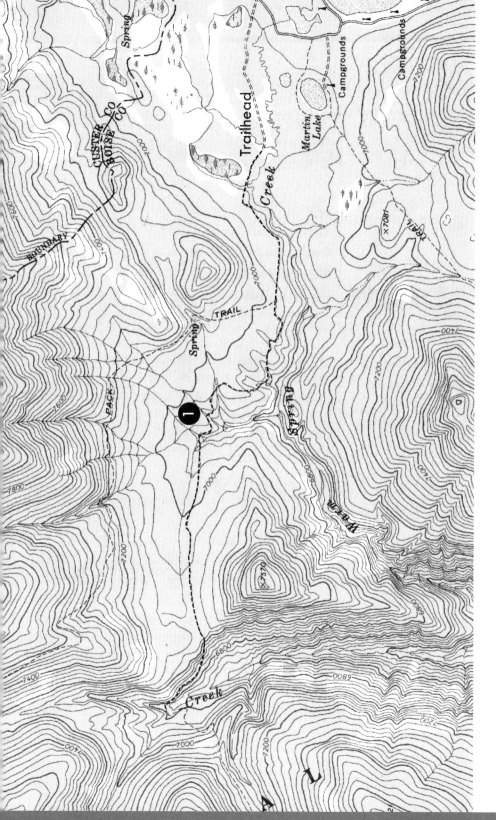

Blue Bunch Mountain

Distance: 8.8 roundtrip

Total elevation gain: 2400 feet

Difficulty: Difficult

Elevation Range: 6520 feet to 8743 feet

Topographic Map: Blue Bunch Mtn.

Time: 4 hours 15 minutes to 6 hours

Distance to trailhead: 29.3 miles

Water Availability: None

Cautionary Advice: *Bring plenty of water and sun protection, most of the hike travels on an open hillside and ridge so it's exposed to the sun. Watch or listen to weather reports before heading out and beware of possible thunderstorm activity. You will also need minor route-finding skills. Bring a USGS topographic map.*

Further Information: Boise National Forest, Lowman Ranger District (208) 259-3361

Coordinates

Trailhead:

North 44d25.644
West 115d17.634

Blue Bunch Mountain:

North 44d28.746
West 115d16.492

Blue Bunch Mountain

The Blue Bunch Mountain trail offers outstanding views, incredible wildflower displays and a trail less traveled. This is a must-do hike for wildflower aficionados and those who cherish vistas. Start out early because so much of the trail is exposed to the sun. The 1987 Deadwood Fire burned much of the forest. It is difficult to see much of the fire damage today as new growth has reclaimed most of the burn area.

As you gain elevation, the inspiring views of the three meadows to the west (Bruce, Poker and Ayers) appear. As you get closer to the top of Blue Bunch Mountain, you're sure to enjoy the electrifying, rugged terrain. A truly unforgettable hike.

Trailhead Directions

From Stanley, drive 21.1 miles east on Highway 21 and turn right on

Warm Lake-Stanley Road towards Bruce Meadow. For 7.8 miles, follow the well-graded dirt road that can occasionally be washboarded. Turn right on road 579A toward the Fir Creek campground. Follow this road 0.4 miles (stay left at all intersections) and the road will dead end at the trailhead.

The Hike

Cross Bear Creek over a bridge and come to a signed junction. The right fork is the Bear Valley Creek Trail (Hike 3). From the junction, turn left and soon the trail turns north through a lodgepole forest. At 0.2 miles arrive at a perch with good views of the creek below. Continue the steep ascent through sagebrush, then enter forest and at 0.7 miles enter an open hillside. Here sagebrush, arrowleaf, yarrow, lupine, and sulphur flower grow rampant. Continue climbing in and out of forest and at 1.0 mile the very scenic Bruce, Ayers and Poker meadows become visible.

At 1.9 miles, the trail flattens out only to begin climbing again at 2.0 miles. The ascent is steep and soon the trail reaches an elevation of 8,050 feet and at 2.5 miles begins traversing across a hillside. Arrive at a small spring at 2.7 miles.

For the next 0.2 miles the trail is non-existent. To find the trail again from the spring, hike directly up the hill, just to the left, or west, of a grouping of trees on the right. At the top of the hill, the terrain flattens and after about 50 yards of hiking, the well-worn trail presents itself again (2.7 miles from the trailhead). For those with a GPS, the coordinates for where the trail becomes obvious again are North 44d27.532 West 115d16.585.

Continue north and at 3.3 miles you'll come to a small knoll. Look to the left for a small rock cairn. Walk to the cairn where more cairns lead around the knoll to where the trail is evident again. The trail continues on the Blue Bunch Ridge with its outstanding views of the rugged wilderness. The trail disappears one last time at 4.0 miles. From here, head up the small hillside at a 45 degree angle and the trail will once again become noticeable at 4.1 miles on a flat area. The trail makes a little dip and a final ascent to the top of Blue Bunch Mountain (8,743 feet).

A rock cairn at the top of the mountain with a small grouping of trees makes a wonderful spot to enjoy a snack and take in the wonderful scenery. To the north: the mountains near the Middle Fork Canyon. To the east: the rugged mountains of the Frank Church. Far off to the southeast: the pointed peaks of the White Clouds. To the south: Cape Horn Mountain. To the southwest: Bear Valley Creek zigzags between Poker and Bruce Meadows.

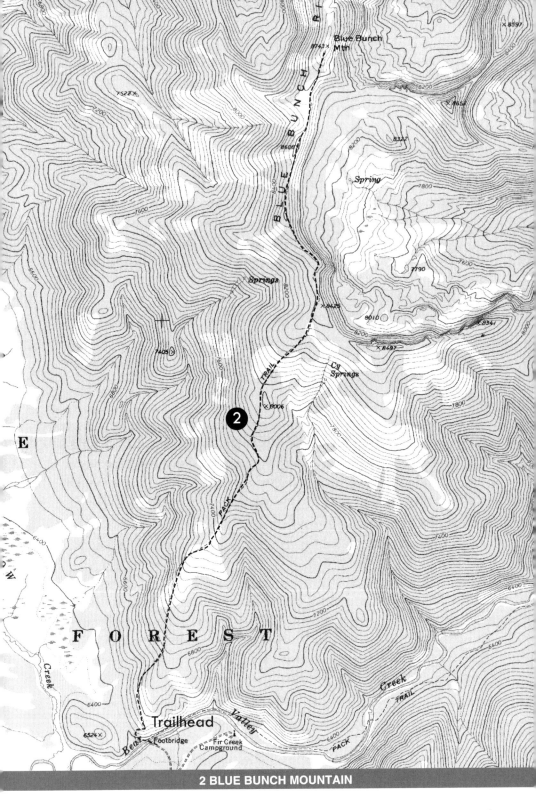

N

Bear Valley Creek Hot Springs

Distance: 7.0 miles roundtrip

Total elevation gain: 550 feet

Difficulty: Moderate

Elevation Range: 6,150 feet to 6,350 feet

Topographic Map: Blue Bunch Mtn, Cape Horn Lakes

Time: 2 hours 45 minutes to 4.0 hours

Distance to trailhead: 29.3 miles

Water Availability: Bear Valley Creek, several side streams

Cautionary Advice: *Crossing Bear Valley Creek can be very dangerous and most likely impassable early in the season. For a better and a safer hike, wait until late summer or early fall. Carry an extra pair of shoes or water sandals because your feet will inevitably get wet. The hot springs has had reports of red spider mites that can bite the skin and leave small red sores. If you find yourself in Bear Valley in the early season, make the hike to the ford for a scenic short hike.*

Further Information: Boise National Forest, Lowman Ranger District (208) 259-3361

Coordinates

Trailhead:

North 44d25.646
West 115d17.631

Bear Valley Creek Hot Springs:

North 44d26.701
West 115d14.370

Bear Valley Creek Hot Springs

Due to the low elevation, this is a good hike to do in early season. But make your final destination the small meadow BEFORE the Bear Valley Creek ford (1.4 miles from the trailhead). The seldom-used trail contains patches of colorful wildflowers. By late summer, the creek flow is low enough to cross the ford. After the ford, the trail stays high above Bear Valley Creek, undulating through a young lodgepole forest and ending up at the hot springs. Hot water tumbles down a rocky hillside into three stair-stepped, crystal-clear pools just large enough for one adult. The dense green forest and small ragged cliffs enhance the scenery.

Trailhead Directions

From Stanley, drive 21.1 miles east on Highway 21 and turn right on Warm Lake-Stanley Road towards Bruce Meadow. For 7.8 miles, follow

One of the hot spring pools near Bear Valley Creek.

the well-graded dirt road that can occasionally be washboarded. Turn right on road 579A toward the Fir Creek campground. Take this road 0.4 miles (stay left at all intersections) until it dead ends at the trailhead.

The Hike

Begin by crossing a well-built footbridge across Bear Valley Creek. The trail splits after crossing the bridge. The left trail travels 4.5 miles to the top of Blue Bunch Mountain (Hike 2). Turn right at this junction and walk along the edge of a talus hillside. At 0.4 miles, cross a tiny stream and at 0.5 miles you'll see the Fir Creek Campground across Bear Valley Creek.

Continue through a small, wildflower-filled meadow. At 0.9 miles the trail parallels the creek within a few feet of its bank. Views up and down the creek are splendid. The trail goes through woods and eventually arrives at a small meadow, a delightful destination and place to turn around if you have small children or want a short hike.

You must cross the creek to continue to the hot springs. Use extreme caution. In early season, the crossing may not be passable due to high water. The creek floor has many slippery large stones. If you decide to cross, use a hiking stick and carry a spare pair of shoes or water sandals.

Once across the creek, the trail remains flat through forest until 1.7 miles. Here it gains 20 feet, crosses a small stream, and enters a remarkably thick forest of tiny lodgepoles. The trail parallels Bear Valley Creek through the forest and crosses another small stream at 2.6 miles. After crossing the stream, the trail makes two switchbacks, continues through dense forest and crosses a third and final side stream at 3.0 miles.

Continue through dense forest, walk along the edge of a talus slope and arrive at the hot springs at 3.5 miles. The hot springs are not marked and it is easy to continue along the trail and pass the springs. To locate the springs, look for footpaths to the left that will lead down the hillside about a tenth of a mile past the rocky talus slope. The hot springs are about 250 feet off of the trail. If you arrive at another crossing of Bear Valley Creek, about 1/4 mile past the hot springs, you've gone too far.

Cape Horn Summit to the Lola Divide

Distance: 7.0 miles roundtrip

Total elevation gain: 2050 feet

Difficulty: Difficult

Elevation Range: 7250 feet to 9200 feet

Topographic Map: Bull Trout Point, Blue Bunch Mountain, Cape Horn Lakes

Time: 3 hours 30 minutes to 5 hours

Water Availability: None

Cautionary Advice: *No reliable water on trail; pack plenty of water. Hike is exposed so bring plenty of sun protection. The upper portions of the hike are along a ridge so turn back if thunderstorm activity threatens.*

Further Information: Salmon-Challis National Forest, Challis-Yankee Fork Ranger District (208) 879-4100

Coordinates

Trailhead coordinates:

North 44d21.848
West 115d16.109

Lola Lake Divide:

North 44d23.474
West 115d14.823

Cape Horn Summit to the Lola Divide

A stunning day hike, the trail begins at Cape Horn Summit and wanders through a burn area from the 1990s. The first 1.5 miles of the burn may not seem like an attractive idea, but the new trees and the beautiful wildflower displays of lupine, penstomen, yarrow, sego lillies, and sulphur flower paint a mind-blowing contrast to the blackened snags. In mid-summer, when wildflowers peak, the area is quite surreal.

Beyond the burn area, the trail winds through beautiful forest. Look to the south for a far-reaching view of an unusual perspective of the Sawtooths. To the west, get a bird's-eye view into three wildlife-rich meadows: Ayers, Bruce and Poker. And to the east, you'll see the rugged mountains in the Challis National Forest. The final destination at the pass has outstanding vistas into the Lola Creek drainage.

Every paradise has its serpent and so has this one ...The hike is steep and lacks reliable water.

Trailhead Directions

From Stanley, take Highway 21 east for 21.1 miles and turn right onto Warm Lake-Stanley Road. Drive 2.9 miles and turn left into a large, undeveloped tree-covered parking area. The trail starts on the opposite side of the road.

The Hike

The hike begins at the base of the summit and heads diagonally across the burned hillside. At 0.2 miles, the trail makes the first switchback, revealing young trees growing from the burn area. Views improve with another switchback at 0.6 miles. After gaining 700 feet from the trailhead, the trail levels around the 1 mile mark. Bunch grass, lupine, sulphur flower and yarrow make this area their home.

The trail climbs again and at 1.6 miles enters a beautiful forest of subalpine fir and lodgepole, making for a wonderful transition out of the burn area.

At 1.8 miles the trail breaks out into a partial burn area with the first views of the majestic Sawtooths off to the right. Views of Bruce, Ayers, and Poker Meadows soon appear on the left. The trail makes five switchbacks working its way to the ridgeline. At 2.7 miles, the trail's grade levels on the ridge. Follow the trail north along the ridge with outstanding views of the Sawtooths to the south, the White Clouds and Salmon Mountains to the east, and the three meadows to the west.

The trail tops out at 9,180 feet and then drops 100 feet behind an unnamed peak (9,310 feet). In midsummer, a marvelous display of penstomen blooms on this section of the trail. The trail emerges from behind the unnamed peak, revealing splendid views down the Lola Creek drainage. The circular upper Lola Lake can be seen glistening below. The hike ends near a cairn marking the intersection of another trail that drops down into the Lola Creek drainage (see Hike 9).

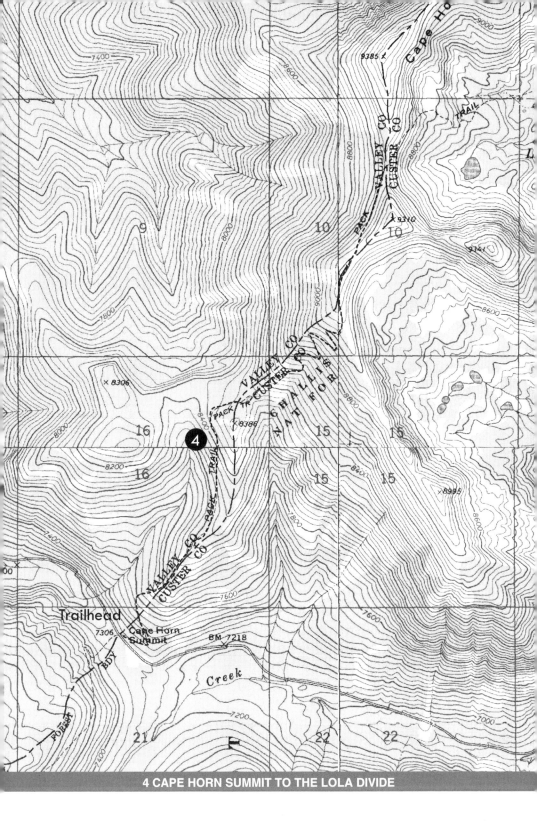

N

Langer Lake/Island Lake/Ruffneck Lake

Distance: 5.2 miles roundtrip

Total elevation gain: 1100 feet

Difficulty: Moderate

Elevation Range: 7100 feet to 8100 feet

Topographic Map: Langer Peak, Cape Horn Lakes

Time: 2 hours 15 minutes to 3 hours 30 minutes

Distance to trailhead: 25.3 miles

Water Availability: Several steams; Langer, Island Lake Ruffneck Lake, several ponds

Cautionary Advice: *None*

Additional Information: Salmon-Challis National Forest, Challis-Yankee Fork Ranger District (208) 879-4100

Coordinates

Trailhead:

North 44d27.962
West 115d06.185

Island Lake:

North 44d28.521
West 115d08.444

Langer/Island Lake/Ruffneck Lake

For those seeking a scenic lake within a relatively close distance to a trailhead, Langer Lake is the place to go. The hike begins with a steep, 500-foot ascent but then becomes quite tame. The hike goes through about 1 mile of burn area from the Fall Creek Fire of 1998. In season, a pleasant display of wildflowers is on display during the first mile of hiking. Thick lodgepole forest and interesting granite outcrops surround Langer Lake.

Another 0.6 miles from Langer Lake is Island Lake and, as one might expect, has a small island near its northeast side. The 250-foot cliffs dipping down to Island Lake's shoreline gives a more rugged look and feel than that of Langer Lake.

And for those comfortable with route finding, the additional hike of 0.3 miles and 200 feet of elevation gain from Island Lake is well worth the

Ruffneck Lake

effort to see the very beautiful and stark Ruffneck Lake.

Trailhead Directions

From Stanley, drive west 18.2 miles on Highway 21. Turn right, heading north, on the well-graded forest road 083. A forest sign on Highway 21 indicates "Seafoam Area, Bradley Boy Scout Camp and the Lola Creek Campground." Turn right and immediately come to another junction. Turn right toward the Seafoam Area, cross Marsh Creek on a bridge and then take the next left on forest road 40008. Follow this road an additional 6.8 miles to the trailhead parking area on the right. The last two miles of the road are washboarded.

The Hike

The trailhead register is located on the opposite side of the road by the Langer Monument. This monument is a memorial for three men who died during World War II while searching for a pilot who had crashed.

This trail begins at 7,100 feet and begins climbing steeply along a hillside. Cross a small stream and then enter a partial burn area. In season, the trail has a wonderful wildflower display including fireweed, lupine, pearly everlasting, penstomen and yarrow. Continue climbing with a switchback at 0.5 miles and reach the top of a ridge at 0.8 miles, 650 feet above the trailhead. From the ridge, impressive views include several unnamed, 8,000 foot-or-higher peaks to the west and southeastern views of the Sawtooths.

From the ridge, begin a short descent and wander through an area where the fire destroyed almost everything. The blackened snags create a somewhat surreal landscape against the backdrop of the large boulders scattered along the trail. Leave the burn area at 1.2 miles. Here the trail makes a short descent, parallels a small creek, and then rises again. The trail then crosses the first of two streams at 1.7 miles and arrives at Langer Lake (8,000 feet) at 2.0 miles.

To get to Island Lake, follow the trail on a ridge above the south side of Langer Lake. Arrive at a signed junction at 2.3 miles from the trailhead. Turning right at this junction leads to Ruffneck Peak (Hike 7) and Upper Finger Lake (Hike 6). Here, turn left towards "lake area." The trail is maintained and obvious, however the Cape Horn lakes quad does not show this section of trail.

Follow this trail around a pond, rise over a knoll, and then descend to a larger second pond. Go around the second pond and then drop about 50 feet down to Island Lake. Note: The Cape Horn Lakes quadrangle has reversed the names of the two lakes, Island Lake and Ruffneck Lake.

For the adventurous and those comfortable with route finding skills, Ruffneck Lake is another 0.3 miles further and a gain of 200 feet. To find Ruffneck Lake, cross the outlet of Island Lake and follow a trail along its shoreline about 20 yards. Here, look to the left for a faint trail that begins heading west up a ridge through forest. The marginal trail is easy to lose. Remember to stay on the ridge above Island Lake and not venture too far left into a gully filled with granite boulders.

As you gain elevation along the ridge, the trail will eventually become more noticeable. The trail soon parallels Ruffneck's outlet (usually dry by mid-summer) and arrives at the aquamarine and very scenic Ruffneck Lake.

6 Upper Finger Lake

Distance: 7.4 miles roundtrip

Total elevation gain: 2100 feet

Difficulty: Difficult

Elevation Range: 7100 feet to 8600 feet

Topographic Map: Langer Peak, Cape Horn Lakes

Time: 3 hours 30 minutes to 5 hours 15 minutes

Distance to trailhead: 25.3 miles

Water Availability: Langer and Upper Finger Lakes, several streams, several ponds

Cautionary Advice: *Upper Finger Lake is located about 1/4 mile off trail, so some route finding skills may be needed. The trail travels through several exposed areas; wear sun protection.*

Additional Information: Salmon-Challis National Forest, Challis-Yankee Fork Ranger District (208) 879-4100

Coordinates

Trailhead:

North 44d27.962
West 115d06.185

Upper Finger Lake:

North 44d29.413
West 115d08.923

Upper Finger Lake

Upper Finger Lake is rarely visited and is quite scenic. The turquoise lake is recessed into a bowl surrounded by gravel and lodgepole pine. The trail to the lake first visits Langer Lake and then heads up to a steep ridge above the Finger Lakes drainage. Views from the ridge are marvelous.

Trailhead Directions

From Stanley, drive west 18.2 miles on Highway 21. Turn right, or north, on the well-graded forest road 083. A forest sign on Highway 21 indicates the "Seafoam Area, Bradley Boy Scout Camp and the Lola Creek Campground." Turn right and immediately come to another junction. Turn right towards the Seafoam Area, cross Marsh Creek on a bridge, and then turn left on forest road 40008. Follow this road an additional 6.8 miles to the trailhead parking area on the right. The last two miles of the road are washboarded.

Upper Finger Lake

The Hike

The trailhead register is located on the opposite side of the road by the Langer Monument. This monument is a memorial to three men who died during World War II searching for a pilot who had crashed.

This trail begins at 7,100 feet and begins climbs steeply along a hillside. Cross a small stream and enter a partial burn area. In season, the trail has a wonderful wildflower display including fireweed, lupine, pearly everlasting, penstomen and yarrow. Continue climbing with a switchback at 0.5 miles and reach the top of a ridge at 0.8 miles, 650 feet above the trailhead. From the ridge, impressive views include several unnamed 8,000-foot and higher peaks to the west and southeastern views of the Sawtooths.

The trail begins a short descent and winds through an area where the fire destroyed almost everything. The blackened snags create a surreal landscape against the backdrop of large boulders scattered along the trail. Leave the burn area at 1.2 miles. Here the trail will make a short descent, parallel a small creek, and then rise again. The trail then crosses two streams beginning at 1.8 miles and arrives at Langer Lake (8,000 feet) at 2.0 miles.

From Langer Lake, the trail climbs gently through forest and arrives at a signed junction in 2.3 miles. The left trail, which is not shown on the Cape Horn Lakes quad, visits several lakes and ponds (Hike 5). Turn right at this junction to Ruffneck Lookout and at 2.5 miles reach yet another junction. The left fork leads to the Ruffneck Peak (Hike 7).

Turn right at this fork towards Fall Creek. Note that the junction and trail are not indicated on the Cape Horn Lakes quad. The trail travels through forest, breaks out into the open, and then begins a very steep ascent to a divide. Reach the divide in 0.5 miles from the junction. The views into the Finger Lakes drainage are superior.

From the divide, descend below an impressive talus slope. Down to the left, the circular Upper Finger Lake can be seen. The lake is not identified on the Cape Horn Lake quad. There is no official route down to the lake. The easiest course to reach the lake is to continue on the trail from the talus slope reentering forest. The lake will no longer be visible due to the density of the trees. Follow the trail about 200 yards. From here, scramble and descend down the left hillside, about 400 yards and 200 feet in elevation. Upper Finger Lake is extremely clear and beckons a swim on a hot summer day.

7 Ruffneck Peak

Distance: 8.4 miles roundtrip

Total Elevation gain: 2400 feet

Difficulty: Difficult

Elevation Range: 7100 feet to 9400 feet

Topographic Map: Langer Peak, Cape Horn Lakes

Time: 4.0 hours to 6.0 hours

Distance to trailhead: 25.3 miles

Water Availability: Several steams; Langer Lake; a couple of ponds

Cautionary Advice: *No water is available the last 1.5 miles of the trail to the lookout. Watch for approaching thunderstorms at the top of Ruffneck Peak.*

Additional Information: Salmon Challis National Forest, Challis-Yankee Fork Ranger District (208) 879-4100

Coordinates

Trailhead:

North 44d27.962
West 115d06.185

Ruffneck Lookout:

North 44d28.904
West 115d09.300

Ruffneck Peak

The panoramic vista from Ruffneck Peak is quite incredible and offers some of the best views described in this book. The fire lookout at the top provides a wonderful location for taking in the ruggedness of the surrounding terrain. Many lakes-including Rocky Lake, Langer Lake, Ruffneck Lake, Island Lake, and several others-shimmer below the peak's edge. The trail leading up to the lookout is also pleasant as it passes through lush forest, boulder fields and along wildflower-scattered hillsides.

Trailhead Directions

From Stanley, drive west 18.2 miles on Highway 21. Turn right, or north, on the well-graded forest road 083. A forest sign on Highway 21 indicates the "Seafoam Area, Bradley Boy Scout Camp and the Lola Creek Campground." Turn right and immediately come to another

View on ridge below Ruffneck Peak.

junction. Turn right towards the Seafoam Area, cross Marsh Creek on a bridge and then turn left on forest road 40008. Follow this road an additional 6.8 miles to the trailhead parking area on the right. The last two miles of the road are washboarded.

The Hike

Follow Hike 5 to Langer Lake. From Langer Lake, the trail climbs gently along the south side of Langer Lake and arrives at a signed junction in 2.3 miles. The left trail, which is not shown on the Cape Horn Lakes quadrangle, visits several lakes and ponds. Turn right at this junction to "Ruffneck L.O." and at 2.5 miles, reach yet another junction. Turn left here through dark forest.

At 2.7 miles, the trail will skirt a pond on the right. This is the last reliable water source on the way to Ruffneck Peak. Leave the woods and begin a 600-foot climb as you enter a boulder field. Begin the first of two switchbacks at 3.3 miles with outstanding views below of Island and Ruffneck Lakes, and then reach a signed junction on a divide at 8,900 feet. The sign indicates the the lookout is 1 mile from here but it is actually 0.7 miles. Views are remarkable.

Turn right at the junction and begin a long traverse up the west side of the mountain. The trail skirts a talus field and begins the first of two switchbacks at 3.9 miles. After the second switchback, the trail turns left, along a ridge with superlative views on both the left and right. Arrive at the mountaintop and lookout at 4.2 miles.

8 Collie Lake

Distance: 7.0 miles

Total elevation gain: 1850 feet

Difficulty: Difficult

Elevation Range: 6450 to 8200 feet

Topographic Map: Cape Horn Lakes

Time: 3 hours 15 minutes to 5 hours

Water Availability: Marsh Creek, multiple streams, Collie Lake

Cautionary Advice: *The trail from the Marsh Creek trail to Collie Lake is not maintained and is not identified on the Cape Horn Lakes USGS map.*

Information: Salmon-Challis National Forest, Challis-Yankee Fork Ranger District (208) 879-4100

Coordinates

Trailhead:

North 44d24.635
West 115d11.102

Collie Lake:

North 44d24.516
West 115d13.437

Collie Lake

Cape Horn Mountain (9,526 feet) provides a wonderful backdrop for Collie Lake. A lush lodgepole forest surrounds its borders, and an 800 foot stair-step cliff drops to its northwest shore. Wildflowers adorn the trail along Collie Creek, including indian paintbrush, arrowleaf balsamroot, arnica, buckwheat, yarrow, mountain bluebell, valerian and penstemon. Although the Cape Horns Lakes topographic map does not show the trail, the well-worn path can be easily followed. Along the Collie Creek drainage, you may have to navigate over a few downed trees. The Collie Lake hike makes an exceptional trail for spotting wildlife including deer, elk, pikas, ground squirrels and marten.

Trailhead Directions

Drive west 18.2 miles on Highway 21. Turn right on the well graded forest road 083. A forest sign on Highway 21 indicates the "Seafoam

Area, Bradley Boy Scout Camp and the Lola Creek Campground."
Turn right and immediately come to another junction. Stay to the left
and go toward the Lola Creek Campground. Follow this road past the
campground, which has bathrooms, to the road's end at 1.5 miles from
Highway 21.

The Hike

The well-maintained trail begins at 6,550 feet and quickly skirts a
talus slope on the left. Listen for the high-pitched alarm call of a pika,
sometimes known as a rock rabbit. They look more like large hamsters
and sometimes can be spotted on top of a rock in the talus field.

After the talus slope, pass a sign marking the Frank Church River of No
Return Wilderness. Marsh Creek can be heard off to the right through
the forest. Continue along the trail, passing two more talus slopes and
then enter lodgepole and subalpine forest.

At 0.6 mile the trail leads up a small ridge above the creek. From this
perch, the ruggedness of this spectacular terrain reveals itself. Go down
to a bridge that crosses Collie Creek at 1.0 mile. From the bridge
continue another 400 feet and look to the left for the trail to Collie Lake.
This junction is NOT SIGNED but look for a blaze on a tree.

From here, the trail gently climbs through forest. At 1.3 miles, the trail
skirts to the left of a talus hillside with striking brown and gray cliffs
above. Begin a climb of 400 feet along the edge of the talus slope,
through forest, and finally to the end of another talus slope. Here the
trail enters a ravine with willows along the creek.

The trail climbs steeply rising 200 feet above the creek. At 2.0 miles,
near the creek, the trail levels then cuts across another talus slope before
entering forest again. Cross a small stream, pass another talus slope and
finally cross one last stream at 2.7 miles.

Now the trail turns northwest and starts a steep climb of 400 feet to a
ford across the outlet stream of Collie Lake. Views of the surrounding
unnamed peaks unfold. Behind you, look for marvelous views deep into
the rugged mountains of the Frank Church Wilderness. After the ford,
the trail continues its steep climb and finally reaches Collie Lake (8,200
feet) at 3.5 miles. In mid-summer, poet shooting star wildflowers border
this exquisite lake.

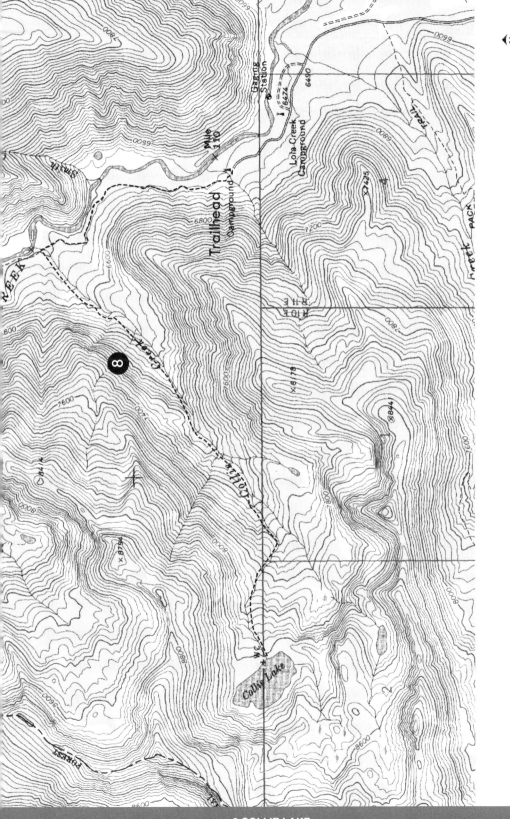

9 Lola Creek to Lola Divide

Distance: 9.0 miles roundtrip to divide (add .35 mile each way and 100 feet of gain to venture to Upper Lola Lake)

Total elevation gain: 2550 feet

Difficulty: Difficult

Elevation Range: 6550 feet to 9100 feet

Topographic Map: Cape Horn Lakes

Time: 4 hours 15 minutes to 6 hours 30 minutes

Distance to trailhead: 18.8 miles

Water Availability: Lola Creek and several unnamed streams that cross the trail

Cautionary Advice: *Route finding skills needed to access upper Lola Lake as there is no trail.*

Additional Information: Salmon-Challis National Forest, Challis-Yankee Fork Ranger District (208) 879-4100

Coordinates
Trailhead:

North 44d24.069
West 115d10.521

Lola Lakes Divide:

North 44d23.474
West 115d14.823

Lola Creek to Lola Divide

An outstanding forest of lodgepole and subalpine fir, spectacular views, opportunities to spot wildlife, solitude and a pristine lake off-trail are just a few highlights on this hike. Although only a little more than a 1/2 mile off of Highway 21, this trail gets few visitors. The ridge on the divide shows 360° views of the White Cloud Mountains, the Salmon Mountains in the Frank Church, Bruce, Poker, and Ayers Meadows, the Sawtooths, and Cape Horn Mountain (9,526 feet).

Trailhead Directions

From Stanley, drive west 18.2 miles on Highway 21. Turn right, north, on the well- graded forest road 083. A forest sign on Highway 21 indicates the "Seafoam Area, Bradley Boy Scout Camp and the Lola Creek Campground." Turn right and immediately come to another junction. Stay to the left and go toward Lola Creek Campground. Follow this road 0.5 miles from Highway

21 and turn left on an unmarked dirt road. Follow this road to its end in 0.1 miles. A sign near the trailhead indicates trail #24.

The Hike

This hike begins with a quick gain of 140 feet in lodgepole forest. The trail levels out for a few minutes and Lola Creek can be heard faintly through the dense forest. A beautiful display of lupine sprinkles this part of the trail. After catching your breath, the trail steepens again and gains another 280 feet by 0.8 miles.

After cresting a tiny knoll, the trail flattens and meanders through dense forest. At 1.2 miles, go around a tiny spring. Continue making gradual elevation gain and at 1.7 miles, approach beautiful Lola Creek.

Those with small children or those out for a short hike will find this to be a pleasant turnaround spot. The area is relatively flat, the creek is clear and numerous trees make a great setting for a picnic.

After crossing Lola Creek, the trail gets very steep. Walk along a hillside scattered with giant boulders and at 1.9 miles, make the first of four switchbacks rising 400 feet above Lola Creek. After the fourth switchback, views of the ridges to the south improve. Continue along the hillside and up the drainage. After two more switchbacks and a little more elevation gain, the trail levels.

From here, the trail continues to gradually rise and comes to a creek crossing at 3.3 miles. After crossing the creek, the trail makes a 60-foot gain to a small saddle. On both sides of the saddle flow small creeks. The trail's grade diminishes and at 3.75 miles (North 44d23.680 West 115d14.156), comes to a small sign on a tree marking "Lola Lakes." The sign is not very obvious and is easy to bypass. From here, no trail leads to the lakes. The sign simply points into the woods.

If you feel comfortable off trail and have the 7.5 quad map, it is 0.35 miles cross country to the upper Lola Lake. The GPS coordinates for the lake are North 44d23.457, West 115d14.379. To find the lake, head in a 45° angle from the trail into the woods. Continue along this angle, using the reddish unnamed peak at 9,341 feet as a beacon. After gaining 100 feet and going up and down over a few small knolls, arrive at the upper Lola Lake. After enjoying the lake, retrace your steps to the trail.

To proceed to the divide, continue along the main trail up a small ridge. The trail veers left from here and at 4.3 miles breaks out of the forest onto an open hillside. To the left are marvelous views of circular upper Lola Lake. The trail is steep, but after a few minutes reach the top of the divide at 4.5 miles and an elevation of 9,100 feet.

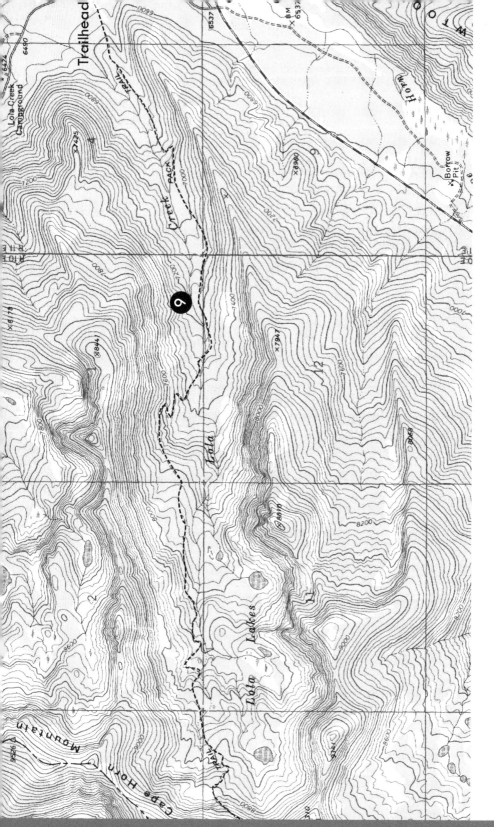

10   Marsh Creek to the Big Hole

Distance: 9.0 miles roundtrip

Total elevation gain: 700 feet

Difficulty: Moderate

Elevation Range: 6450 feet to 6200 feet

Topographic Map: Cape Horn Lakes

Time: 3 hours 30 minutes to 5 hours

Distance to Trailhead: 19.7 miles

Water Availablility: Plenty along Marsh Creek

Cautionary Advice: *Get an early start on summer as this hike is at a low elevation and can be hot by mid-day.*

Information: Salmon Challis National Forest, Challis-Yankee Fork Ranger District (208) 879-4100

Coordinates

Trailhead:

North 44d24.640
West 115d11.096

Big Hole:

North 44d26.999
West 115d13.849

Marsh Creek to the Big Hole

The Marsh Creek trail undulates through a majestic canyon and ends at the confluence of Marsh Creek and Bear Creek. The confluence is the beginning of the Middle Fork of the Salmon River, which is heralded as one of the great whitewater rafting adventures in the United States. Just beyond the confluence is the Big Hole, which is a deep, dark-blue pool along the Middle Fork of the Salmon.

Unlike most trails in this book, this hike starts at a higher elevation than it ends. Small children will enjoy the first mile of this hike because it is relatively flat and ends at a bridge that spans Marsh Creek. Wildlife spotting opportunities are abundant and may include elk, deer, ground squirrels, pikas, chipmunks and marten.

Early summer sees a profusion of wildflowers, including indian paintbrush, arnica, buttercup, arrowleaf balsamroot and gilia white. Because of the low

The Big Hole along the Middle Fork of the Salmon.

elevation and the bridge across Marsh Creek, the trail is an excellent choice in early season.

Trailhead Directions

Drive west 18.2 miles on Highway 21. Turn right (north) on the well-graded forest road 083. There will be a forest sign on Highway 21 indicating the "Seafoam Area, Bradley Boy Scout Camp and the Lola Creek Campground." Turn right and follow the sign to Lola Creek Campground. Go past the campground, which has bathrooms, to the road's end at 1.5 miles.

The Hike

The well-maintained trail begins at 6,450 feet. Sign in at the trailhead register and skirt a talus slope on the left. This is a wonderful spot to hear the high-pitched alarm call of a pika, also known as a rock rabbit. They look more like large hamsters and sometimes can be spotted on top of rocks in the boulder field.

After the talus slope, pass a sign indicating the Frank Church River of No Return Wilderness. Marsh Creek becomes audible through the forest to the right. Continue along the trail, passing two more talus slopes, and then enter lodgepole and subalpine forest.

At 0.6 mile from the trailhead, the trail leads up a small ridge above the creek. From this perch, the ruggedness of this spectacular terrain begins to reveal itself. Descend to a bridge that crosses Collie Creek at 1.0 mile.

Cross the bridge and soon come to another bridge that spans Marsh Creek. This is a wonderful spot for a picnic and a great turnaround (1.2 mile one way) with small children. There is a small, white-sand beach with plenty of shade. Be careful of the current in early season.

After crossing the bridge, bypass another talus slope with opportunities to spot pikas and indulge in wild raspberries if your timing is good. At 1.4 miles, gain another small ridge that rises above Marsh Creek. From here, descend into lodgepole forest again with a foot step crossing of Allen Creek at 1.6 miles. Soon cross a small bridge that spans fast-flowing Walker Creek.

Continue through forest beside Marsh Creek and at 2.3 miles begin a steep rise where the trail has been dynamited into the hillside. Views up and down the canyon are memorable. At 2.5 miles, enter the forest again and cross two creeks at 2.8 miles and 3.4 miles, respectively. In this area, the valley floor is a little wider and the creek snakes through the canyon.

After the two creek crossings, the trail pulls away from Marsh Creek for a bit. The trail rejoins the creek just before bisecting a scenic talus slope at 3.75 miles and begins a steady rise above the creek. Once again, views are impressive. The trail stays high above the creek with a marvelous array of hillside wildflowers in early season. Soon the trail will begin descending and come to a junction for the Bear Valley Creek Trail and the Middle Fork Trail at 4.3 miles.

There is no official trail to the Big Hole. There are two options to find the Big Hole. The first is to go straight on the Middle Fork Trail to the next junction, which is only about 700 feet further. At this junction, turn left and follow the trail for a minute or two until footpaths are visible off to the right leading down to the river and the Big Hole. The second option is to turn left at the first junction onto the Bear Valley Creek Trail. Hike about 25 yards and then look for footpaths off to the right heading through the open forest. The footpaths will lead down to the Big Hole.

N

Marsh Creek/Big Hole/Middle Fork of the Salmon

Distance: 14.6 miles roundtrip

Total elevation gain: 1350 feet

Difficulty: Very Difficult

Elevation Range: 6450 feet to 6100 feet

Topographic Map: Cape Horn Lakes

Time: 5 hours 30 minutes to 8 hours 15 minutes

Distance to Trailhead: 19.7 miles

Water Availablility: Plenty along Marsh Creek and the Middle Fork of the Salmon, several side streams

Cautionary Advice: *Get an early start during summer as this hike is at a low elevation and can be hot by mid-day.*

Information: Salmon Challis National Forest, Challis-Yankee Fork Ranger District (208) 879-4100

Coordinates

Trailhead coordinates:

North 44d24.640
West 115d11.096

Viewpoint:

North 44d28.686
West 115d13.486

Marsh Creek/Big Hole/Middle Fork of the Salmon

After leaving the spectacular Marsh Creek drainage, this trail turns north and continues along the Middle Fork of the Salmon. This canyon is a little wider than the canyon along Marsh Creek and offers more expansive views of the rugged terrain. The trail undulates from a level even with the river to as much as 400 feet above. From the high segments, the vistas are easily worth the additional couple miles of hiking. In addition, the trail passes several scenic talus areas and offers additional wildflower and wildlife viewing opportunities.

Trailhead Directions

Drive west 18.2 miles on Highway 21. Turn right (north) on the well graded forest road 083. There will be a forest sign on Highway 21 indicating the "Seafoam Area, Bradley Boy Scout Camp and the Lola Creek Campground." Turn right and follow the sign to Lola Creek

Above the Middle Fork of the Salmon River.

Campground. Go past the campground, which has bathrooms, to the road's end at 1.5 miles.

The Hike

Follow Hike 10 to the Big Hole. At the first signed junction near the Big Hole, turn right and head north along the Middle Fork Trail. Quickly arrive at another signed junction for the Bear Valley Creek trail. Continue straight along the Middle Fork and at 4.6 miles from the trailhead the trail will rise steeply above the creek. Views of the swift Middle Fork of the Salmon River some 100 feet below are splendid.

The trail now descends and skirts the edge of a talus hillside. Enter forest at 5.0 miles and then descend to the river's edge at 5.4 miles. Here, the Middle Fork nearly touches the rocky trail. This is an especially scenic section of trail with the steep granite walls shouldering the right-hand side of the trail.

The trail now passes an intermittent stream and then rises 100 feet. At 6.3 miles, enter a relatively flat area with a couple of footpaths leading down to the river's edge. Shortly, the trail starts to rise for the last time on this hike. Cross Jose Creek at 6.9 miles and and break out of tree cover at 7.2 miles. The trail reenters forest at 7.3 miles, perched some 400 feet above the river. Views of the surrounding area are superlative. This is the end point for this hike. Following the trail further leads back down to the river and eventually to the junction with the Fall Creek Trail.

Marten/Kelly Lakes

Distance: 7.8 miles roundtrip (Marten Lake)

9.2 miles roundtrip (Kelly Lake)

Total elevation gain: 700 Feet (Marten Lake)

1000 feet (Kelly Lake)

Difficulty: Moderate

Elevation Range: 6850 feet to 7850 feet

Topographic Map: Elk Meadow, Banner Summit

Time: 3 hours 30 minutes to 5 hours 14 minutes (Kelly Lake)

Distance to Trailhead: 9.4 miles

Water Availability: Trap Creek, Marten and Kelly lakes, several side streams

Cautionary Advice: *Because the lakes lie just to the north of a rocky divide, the snow melts a little later than the altitude might suggest.*

Additional information: Sawtooth National Recreation Area (208) 774-3000

Coordinates
Trailhead:

North 44d19.682
West 115d07.207

Kelly Lake:

North 44d16.930
West 115d09.446

Marten/Kelly Lakes

The goals of this particular hike are two pristine lakes. The lakes are located in the northern section of the Sawtooths. Because of their location off of Highway 21 and the fact that the trail does not journey into the high alpine country of the Sawtooths, these lakes get relatively little use. You have a good chance for solitude.

A splendid rocky peak and a dense forest shoulder Marten Lake at 7,556 feet. The slightly more picturesque Kelly Lake at 7,842 feet has an unnamed peak at 8,371 feet spilling into its southern shore. In addition to the scenery of the lakes, attractive terrain and wildflowers shoulder many sections of the trail.

Trailhead Directions

From Stanley, drive west 8.6 miles on Highway 21 and turn left on a small dirt road, forest road 199, with a brown sign that says, "Marten Lake 8." Follow this easily-navigated dirt road 0.4 miles. There is a small parking area to the right. If you have 4-wheel drive or a high-clearance vehicle, drive over a 20-foot stretch of rough road and go another 0.4 miles to the trailhead on the left. If you parked at the small parking area, hike the road 0.4 miles to the trailhead, adding another 0.8 miles to the total distance of the hike.

The Hike

The first section of the trail weaves its way through lodgepole forest. Trap Creek can be heard off to the left, at 0.5 miles. Continue another 0.2 miles and enter a small meadow. In early and mid-season, the meadow contains numerous wildflowers, including avens, primrose, american bistort and sheep sorrel. At 1 mile, leave the meadow and arrive at a small pond. This is a nice spot for a picnic and turnaround if you have limited time or small children.

Continue hiking through forest, making gradual elevation gain. At 2.3 miles, cross a very scenic meadow with an open hillside. A wonderful display of wildflowers blooms in early to mid-season. Here an unnamed creek in the meadow, makes a logical destination for an abbreviated 4.6-mile roundtrip hike.

After leaving the meadow the trail begins a steep climb. In early season, the hills are covered with arrowleaf balsamroot and the large yellow flowers give an added depth to the beauty of the mountains. Continue making gradual elevation gain and the trail will flatten out at 3.2 miles. Cross a small stream and at 3.3 miles cross a long platform bridge, with two more bridges quickly following.

At 3.6 miles, the trail comes within a few yards of Trap Creek. Climb another 0.3 miles and 160 feet of gain and arrive at a signed junction. To the right, find trails for Elk and Bench Creek. Go left along Trap creek another 100 yards to the northeast shore of Marten Lake (7,556 feet).

To get to Kelly Lake, cross the outlet stream on a small log jam. Enter forest and cross a small stream at 4.3 miles from the trailhead. To the left are superb views of the drainage leading down to the trailhead. In the far distance, mountain peaks and ridges rise in the Frank Church Wilderness. Continue another 0.3 miles, and after crossing the outlet stream reach delightful Kelly Lake (7,842 feet), 4.6 miles from the trailhead.

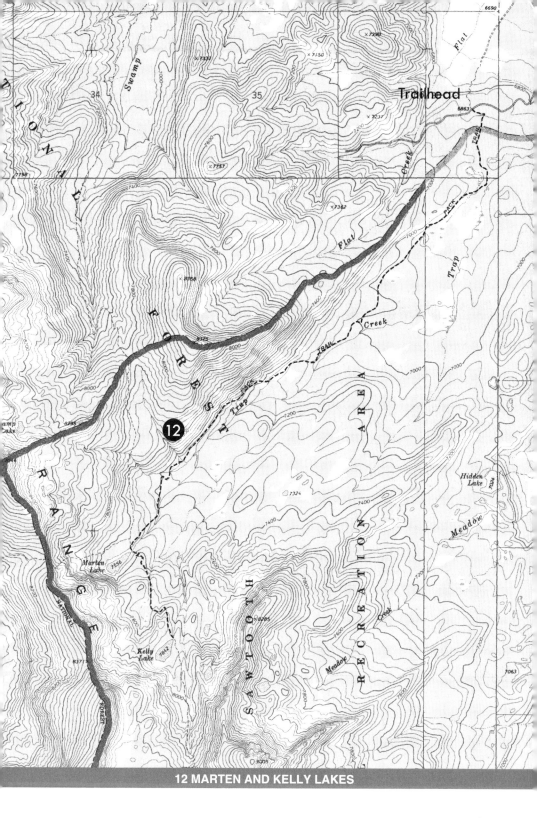

Trailhead

12

N

13 Elk Meadow

Distance: 5.0 miles roundtrip

Total elevation gain: 250 feet

Difficulty: Easy

Elevation Range: 6700 feet to 6900 feet

Topographic Map: Elk Meadow

Time: 1 hour 45 minutes to 2 hours 45 minutes

Distance to trailhead: 10.1 miles

Water Availability: Plenty along Elk Creek

Cautionary Advice: *Trail travels in and out of forest. Bring sun protection; also be sure to bring mosquito repellent for Elk Meadow. Because the trail was rerouted in 1995, the trail on the 1972 Elk Meadow quad is not accurate.*

Further Information: Sawtooth National Recreation Area (208) 774-3000

Coordinates

Trailhead:

North 44d17.289
West 115d04.283

Elizabeth Lake:

North 44d15.881
West 115d09.015

Elk Meadow

Beautiful Elk Meadow stretches 2.5 miles long and expands, at its widest, over ½ mile. Forest-covered mountains and many unnamed rocky peaks surround the meadow. Wildflowers grow rampant in June and early July. The penstomen display alone makes it worth the trip. The meadow appears particularly magical at sunset when the sun sinks behind the Sawtooths.

Several crystal-clear streams snake their way across the marshy flat. Sand hill cranes can usually be seen during the summer months.

Because of the low elevation, the trail is accessible in early season. It is also a splendid hike to enjoy with children due to the minimal elevation gain.

Trailhead Directions

From Stanley, drive 8.5 miles and turn left onto the well-graded forest road 614. Drive 0.3 miles and take the left arm at a "Y" intersection onto Elk Meadow Road. Follow this well-graveled dirt road to the end, 1.6 miles from Highway 21.

The Hike

The trail to Elk Meadow begins in dense forest and quickly crosses a well-built bridge over Elk Creek. After crossing the creek, turn right up an old roadbed. This is the only significant elevation gain to Elk Meadow. After an 180-foot climb, arrive at a signed junction to Elk Meadow. Turn right on the maintained trail.

At 0.7 miles, the trail skirts a small meadow. This is a good spot for a picnic and a turnaround for those hiking with small children. In mid-summer, the children can wade in the crystal-clear creek. From here the trail stays relatively flat wandering in and out of partial forest until arriving at the northeast side of the meadow at 1.9 miles. The trail turns south through trees and emerges out into the open at 2.1 miles.

When you come out of the forest, keep your eyes and ears open for sand hill cranes in the meadow. Also, if you are hiking in June to early July, when the wildflowers are blooming, be sure to notice the thousands of penstomen in various shades of purple, especially in the middle and southern part of the meadow.

Once out of the trees, the trail heads south to a signed junction at 2.5 miles, which is the end of this hike. The trail to Elizabeth Lake turns right at this junction and is described in Hike 15.

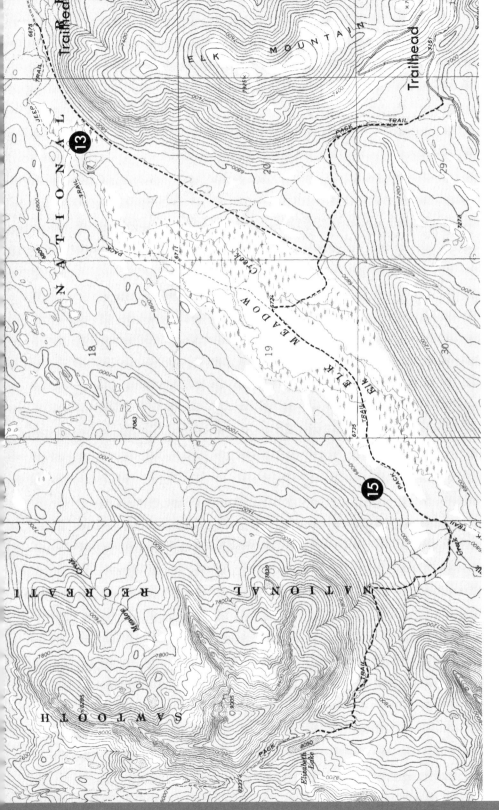

Lady Face And Bridal Veil Falls

Distance: 4.8 miles roundtrip (Lady Face Falls)

7.9 miles roundtrip (Bridal Veil Falls)

Total elevation gain: 350 feet

Difficulty: Easy (Lady Face Falls)

Moderate (Bridal Veil Falls)

Elevation Range: 6500 feet to 6850

Topographic Map: Stanley Lake

Time: 1 hour 45 minutes to 2 hours 30 minutes (Lady Face Falls)

2 hours 45 minutes to 4 hours (Bridal Veil Falls)

Distance to Trailhead: 8.6 miles

Water Availability: Stanley Lake, Stanley Lake Creek

Cautionary Advice: *The steep and slippery banks above Lady Face Falls can be dangerous. Use caution around this area. Be sure to hold your children's hands at the falls. The trail from Lady Face Falls to Bridal Veil Falls requires a ford of Stanley Lake Creek. In early season, this crossing can be very treacherous and may not be possible.*

Additional Information: Sawtooth National Recreation Area (208) 774-3000

Coordinates

Trailhead:

North 44d14.651
West 115d03.987

Best view area near Bridal Veil Falls:

North 44d12.709
West 115d06.109

Lady Face and Bridal Veil Falls

This hike begins near Stanley Lake and proceeds through a delightful meadow filled with a variety of wildflowers, including fleabane, groundsel, penstemon, cinquefoil, larkspur, agoseris and yarrow. Beyond the meadow, the trail wanders through lodgepole forest and finally to an unofficial footpath that descends 0.1 miles to the banks above Lady Face Falls.

Past Lady Face Falls, the hike is relatively flat with scenic views of granite and forested mountainsides along the drainage of Stanley Lake Creek. The final destination is Bridal Veil Falls, which tumbles from the lowest of the Hanson Lakes down the mountainside. This hike also contains a side trail that offers a scenic destination for those with children.

Trailhead Directions

Drive 4.8 miles from Stanley and turn left onto road 455 towards Stanley Lake. Drive 3.5 miles on the paved road to an intersection just north of Stanley Lake. Turn right and drive 0.1 miles to the large parking area on the left. To find the trailhead, follow the small path to the left of the parking area and follow it to the dirt road. Turn right on the dirt road and proceed to the trailhead 0.2 miles from the parking area.

Note: Hike mileage and times have been computed from the parking area.

The Hike

The hike from the trailhead begins alongside the crystal-clear waters of Stanley Lake Creek. At 0.7 miles, the trail breaks out of the forest into an open meadow. In midseason this meadow has many wildflowers, including yarrow, penstomen, cinquefoil, and larkspur. Go through the meadow on a raised footpath, built to avoid damage to the wet meadow, with outstanding views of McGown Peak (9,860 feet) and other smaller unnamed peaks.

At 1.1 miles, enter lodgepole forest and at 1.5 miles, come to a signed junction. For those with small children who are seeking a spot for a picnic, turn left and at 0.1 miles enter the official Sawtooth Wilderness. Hike through forest another 0.1 miles and arrive at Stanley Lake Creek. This is a wonderful setting for a picnic with a view of McGown Peak in the background.

To continue to Lady Face Falls, continue straight at the junction. At 1.9 miles, skirt the edge of a small meadow on the right and at 2.1 miles begin ascending. After a gain of a little less than 300 feet, the trail flattens on top of a small knoll at 2.4 miles. Look to the left on a tree for a sign that says "Lady Face Falls." To go down to the falls, follow the footpath down about 0.1 miles to the banks above the falls.

To continue on to Bridal Veil Falls, hike from the turn off to Lady Face Falls another 0.3 miles to the crossing of Stanley Lake Creek. This crossing may not be possible in early season because the creek runs swift and high and can be very dangerous. If the creek is passable, cross and hike through forest and at 3.6 miles from the trailhead, come to a "Y" in the trail with a footpath leading to the right. For the best viewing options, go past the "Y" and hike straight ahead another 0.2 miles to a sign on a tree for Bridal Veil Falls. Turn right at this "Y" on a footpath and hike about 250 feet to an opening in the forest along Stanley Lake Creek for one of the best views of the falls. Several paths lead up to the falls but the views actually deteriorate the closer you get and are not worth the time to continue.

Trailhead

Inlet
Campground

BM 653

31 x7448

32

33

TRAIL

JEEP

BM
6582 x

6539

Lady Face
Falls

Creek

BM 6831 x

14

6600

6800

7200

7444

8000

C H A

x 9115

8575

9248

8350

BOUNDARY

BM 6860 x

8575

8575

Bridal Veil
Falls

7800

Lake

9660

McGown
Peak

8609

9820

WILDERNESS

JEEP

N   A   T   I   O   N   A   L

9604

BM 6967 x

Stanley
Trail

7200

9709 x

14 LADY FACE AND BRIDAL VEIL FALLS

N

Elk Meadow/Elizabeth Lake

Distance: 9.8 miles

Difficulty: Difficult

Total elevation gain: 1800 feet

Elevation Range: 6700 feet to 8100 feet

Topographic Map: Elk Meadow, Banner Summit

Time: 4 1/4 hours to 6 1/4 hours

Distance to trailhead: 10.1 miles

Water Availability: Streams in Elk Meadow, Elizabeth Lake

Cautionary Advice: *Bring sun protection and mosquito repellent for Elk Meadow. The trail across Elk Meadow is faint and difficult to follow. You'll need a pair of sandals or water shoes to keep your boots dry to cross the boggy water near Elk Meadow Creek. Once across the meadow, the trail is well worn to Elizabeth Lake.*

Additional Information: Sawtooth National Recreation Area (208) 774-1116

Coordinates

Trailhead:

North 44d15.249
West 115d04.770

Elizabeth Lake:

North 44d15.881
West 115d09.015

Elk Meadow/Elizabeth Lake

Beautiful Elk Meadow is about 2 1/2 miles long and 1/2 mile wide. Forest-covered mountains and many unnamed rocky peaks surround the meadow. Wildflowers grow rampant in June and early July. The penstomen display alone is worth the trip. When the sun sinks behind the Sawtooths, the meadow feels magical. The meadow makes a good turnaround spot for a 2.4 mile roundtrip hike with children.

Dark green Elizabeth Lake lies at an elevation of 8090 feet. Lodgepole pine, subalpine firs and a few small granite cliffs surround the lake. Top-notch views can be seen from a ridge just prior to the lake of the surrounding mountains. This hike is the shorter alternative to reach Elk Meadow (Hike 13), but it does require a 350-foot climb on the return.

Crossing Elk Meadow, where the trail is overgrown and nonexistent in some sections, can be a challenge in reaching Elizabeth Lake. Fortunately, the Forest Service has placed a couple of signs in the meadow to help with navigation. Once across the meadow, the trail up to the lake is very obvious. Although the trail from Elk Meadow to Elizabeth Lake is scenic, it is also very steep—so plan for a vigorous workout.

Trailhead Directions

Drive 4.8 miles from Stanley and turn left onto road 455 towards Stanley Lake. Drive 3.5 miles on the paved road to an intersection just north of Stanley Lake. Turn right onto the dirt road and drive 1.8 miles further to a large parking area on the left.

The Hike

The hike begins in dense forest of subalpine firs and lodgepole pines on the Elk Mountain Loop Trail. The trail descends after rising to a flat ridge. The trail's descent steepens at 0.5 mile and then flattens at 0.9 miles. Cross a tiny meadow filled with wildflowers. Arrive at a signed junction at 1.2 miles. This junction is not shown of the Elk Meadow 7.5 quad. Turning right at this junction leads to the trailhead for Hike 13.

At the junction, continue straight, or west, into Elk Meadow. Cross a small stream and soon the trail disappears for about 20 yards into the boggy section of the meadow. The water is usually about a foot deep, so have an extra pair of shoes or prepare for wet boots. After crossing this area, come immediately to the crossing of Elk Creek; it may be up to your knees, depending on snowmelt.

After crossing the creek, a signed junction (North 44d16.010 West 115d06.086) 1.4 miles from the trailhead points to the lower Elk Meadow and the upper Elk Meadow. Although this junction is signed, it is almost comical because there is little sign of a trail. This is where the trail can get tricky. The grass may obscure any note of a trail. Go south to southwest, heading towards the far end of the meadow, for a little over a 1/2 mile.

At 2.0 miles there is another sign (North 44d15.675 West 115d06.640) in the middle of the meadow that has arrows and the word "trail." From here, the trail is faint but can be noticed by looking carefully. Head southwest towards the edge of the forest. Just before reaching the forest, turn left and head due south without going into the trees. Soon the trail becomes visible again. At 2.7 miles, the trail enters the forest again and reaches another signed junction for Marten Lake at 3.1 miles.

Turn right into the forest and at 3.4 miles begin a very steep ascent. Get ready for a good workout, because the trail climbs 1150 feet over the next 1.5 miles. The trail goes almost straight up with only a couple of switchbacks. Fortunately, the forest is thick and provides ample shade.

After a more than 900-foot climb, the trail levels out for a few minutes 4.3 miles from the trailhead. Begin a final ascent to the lake with a steep hillside climb and two switchbacks. The trail tops out on a knoll and then veers to the right. Elizabeth Lake is about 20 yards to the left, although it cannot be seen due to a knoll. A hard-to-find, faded sign on a tree indicates Elizabeth Lake.

16 Alpine Lake

Distance: 8.0 miles roundtrip

Total elevation gain: 1200 feet

Difficulty: Moderate

Elevation Range: 6700 feet to 7900 feet

Topographic Map: Stanley Lake

Time: 2 hours 15 minutes to 5 hours

Distance to trailhead: 5.8 miles

Water Availability: Iron Creek, Alpine Lake

Cautionary Advice: *This is one of the most popular trailheads in the Sawtooth Wilderness. Mid-week hiking is highly recommended during the busy summer months.*

Information: Sawtooth National Recreation Area (208) 774-3000

Coordinates
Trailhead:

North 44d11.920
West 115d00.841

Alpine Lake:

North 44d11.040
West 115d03.243

Alpine Lake

A beautiful glaciated bowl holds Alpine Lake (7,823 feet). The lodgepole forest and granite slabs that surround the lake make an excellent lunch spot. The trail winds its way up to the lake through scenic forest, skirts beautiful flower-filled meadows, and finally climbs a forested hillside to the lake. There are outstanding views of many unnamed granite peaks in the official wilderness area (1.1 miles). Just beyond the wilderness boundary, Iron Creek flows through a meadow that makes for an ideal turnaround location for those with children.

Trailhead Directions

From Stanley, drive 2.6 miles west on Highway 21 and turn left onto Iron Creek Road, forest road 619. Continue on the dirt road 3.2 miles to the large trailhead parking area on the right. Restrooms are available.

The Hike

The trail begins at 6,700 feet, meandering through lodgepole and subalpine fir forest. At 0.5 miles the trail will parallel Iron Creek and cross a platform bridge across marshy ground. Begin a gradual ascent and at 1.1 miles enter the wilderness boundary. From July 1 through Labor Day, dogs must be on leash beyond this point.

Go another 100 yards past the wilderness boundary to a signed junction for Marshall Lake and Sawtooth Lake. If you have small children or you want a short hike, Iron Creek and a very pristine meadow offer gorgeous views and an ideal picnic spot just a few yards from the junction.

To continue to Alpine Lake, turn right towards Sawtooth Lake. The trail will skirt the edge of the meadow and at 1.7 miles come to another signed junction (7,100 feet). Turn left here. The trail steepens, improving the views of the surrounding unnamed peaks.

Begin the first of four switchbacks and continue through woods heading for the towering peaks ahead. At 2.9 miles, emerge into a small, flower-filled meadow and cross a log jam over the outlet stream of Sawtooth Lake. This meadow offers another ideal destination for a short hike.

The trail quickly crosses the meadow and begins a series of fifteen switchbacks snaking way up the mountainside. At 3.9 miles, arrive at another signed junction. Turn left, and descend about 50 feet and 0.1 miles to beautiful Alpine Lake. This emerald green lake is set in a glacial bowl. Take in all of the spectacular scenery from the flat granite slabs.

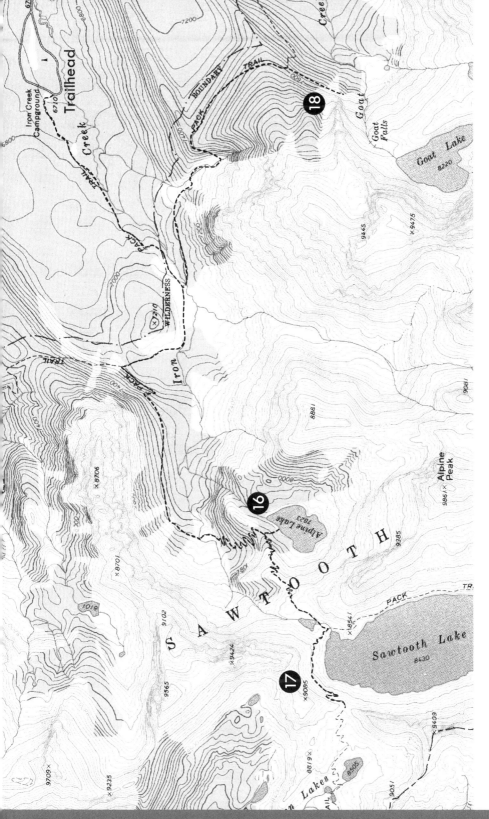

Sawtooth Lake to Sawtooth/McGown Divide

Distance: 11.5 miles roundtrip

Total elevation gain: 2200 feet

Difficulty: Difficult

Elevation Range: 6700 feet to 8800 feet

Topographic Map: Stanley Lake

Time: 5.0 hours to 7 hours 30 minutes

Distance to trailhead: 5.8 miles

Water Availability: Alpine and Sawtooth Lakes, several side streams and Iron Creek

Cautionary Advice: *The winds can be ruthless blowing off of Sawtooth Lake. Be prepared with a wind breaker and a light jacket. Be cautious of approaching thunderstorms on the exposed ridge above Sawtooth Lake. This trailhead is very busy on weekends.*

Additional Information: Sawtooth National Recreation Area (208) 774-3000

Coordinates

Trailhead:

North 44d11.920
West 115d00.841

Divide:

North 44d10.684
West 115d04.213

Sawtooth Lake to Sawtooth/McGown Divide

Just a mile beyond Alpine Lake sits Sawtooth Lake. Sawtooth Lake is one of the most scenic lakes in the Sawtooth Wilderness. The sheer size of the clear sparkling lake-nearly 170 acres-is breathtaking. The lake is shouldered by two outstanding peaks, Mount Regan (10,190 feet) and the massive Alpine Peak (9,861 feet), along with many other unnamed peaks close to 9,400 feet.

The trail to the lake is compelling, making no less than 15 switchbacks to climb the rocky walls to the west of Alpine Lake. Views of the surrounding peaks with their jagged pinnacles are spectacular.

From Sawtooth Lake, the trail rises 300 feet to the pass between Sawtooth Lake and the McGown Lakes. Views from this location will long be remembered.

Sawtooth Lake on the trail near the Sawtooth/McGown Divide.

Trailhead Directions

From Stanley, drive west on Highway 21 for 2.6 miles and turn left on Iron Creek Road, forest road 619. Continue on the dirt road 3.2 miles to the large trailhead parking area on the right. Restrooms are available.

The Hike

Follow Hike 16 to the junction just before Alpine Lake. Turn right at the junction. The trail rises with scenic views of Alpine Lake below. After a few more minutes the many serrated unnamed peaks to the north become visible. The city of Stanley can be seen far below in the valley.

After completing 15 switchbacks, the trail grade diminishes as it snakes up to a flat area. Just beyond this stretch of trail, an idyllic lake becomes visible off to the right.

The trail continues to the left of the unnamed lake, crosses the outlet creek for Sawtooth Lake on logs, and makes a little rise to another junction just a few yards from Sawtooth Lake. The left trail crosses the outlet stream again and wanders along the eastern shore of the lake, inviting you to explore.

For out-of-this-world views, turn right at the junction and go toward the McGown Lakes. The trail rises above the unnamed lake, makes three switchbacks and begins a traverse along a rocky slope above Sawtooth Lake. Make two final switchbacks and arrive at the 8,800-foot divide.

18 Goat Falls

Distance: 6.8 miles roundtrip

Total elevation gain: 1050 feet

Difficulty: Moderate

Elevation Range: 6700 feet to 7650 feet

Topographic Map: Stanley Lake

Time: 2 hours 45 minutes to 4 hours 15 minutes

Distance to trailhead: 5.8 miles

Water Availability: Iron Creek, Goat Creek, a couple of small side streams

Cautionary Advice: *The Iron Creek Trailhead is one of the most popular and hiked trails in the Sawtooths. Avoid summer weekends.*

Additional Information: Sawtooth National Recreation Area (208) 774-3000

Coordinates

Trailhead:

North 44d11.920
West 115d00.841

Goat Falls:

North 44d10.690
West 115d00.842

Goat Falls

Most people who use this trail tend to hike to Alpine and Sawtooth lakes, leaving moderate traffic en route to Goat Falls. Goat Falls cascades down along the granite wall below Granite Lake. Wildflowers fill the open hillside. This hike has wonderful views of Williams Peak (10,635 feet). As a bonus, south of Goat Falls another unnamed waterfall tumbles down the granite slopes. The forested trail provides good sun protection and has several sections of scenic wildflowers.

Trailhead Directions

From Stanley, drive west on Highway 21 for 2.6 miles and turn left onto Iron Creek Road, forest road 619. Follow the road 3.2 miles, and turn right into the parking area for the Iron Creek Trailhead. Restrooms are available.

The Hike

From the Iron Creek trailhead, head southwest along the main trail through lodgepole and subalpine forest. At 0.5 miles, the relatively flat trail parallels Iron Creek. Cross a marshy area on a platform bridge and then begin a 200-foot climb to the wilderness boundary. Proceed another 100 yards to a signed junction. The trail to the right leads to Alpine and Sawtooth lakes (Hike 16). Turn left at this junction towards Marshall Lake.

Goat Falls

The trail crosses Iron Creek on a couple of downed trees. Go through shaded forest and at 1.5 miles cross a small stream. Here the trail begins a 600-foot ascent. This ascent starts with a switchback and then goes up a ravine on an open hillside. Wildflowers include lupine, sego lily, penstomen and indian paintbrush.

The trail makes another switchback and returns into forest. Make one final switchback and then head southeast before topping out at 7,650 feet. Continue on level ground to an unmarked junction at 2.9 miles. The Alpine Way trail heads down the hill to the left and eventually leads to Marshall Lake. To go to the falls, go straight along an open hillside. Wildflowers fill this stretch of trail. In the horizon, an unnamed waterfall can be seen tumbling down the granite slopes to the south.

At 3.3 miles, the trail dead ends under a small grouping of lodgepole trees. Here several footpaths lead in various directions. For the best views of the falls, descend the left footpath about 100 feet in elevation and 175 yards in distance to an open clearing before the creek. Below the falls are many large boulders, offering outstanding picnic spots to take in the outstanding scenery.

West Fork of Yankee Creek/Lightning Creek

Distance: 13.0 miles roundtrip

Total elevation gain: 1900 feet

Difficulty: Difficult

Elevation Range: 6550 feet to 7250 feet

Topographic Map: East Basin Creek, Mt. Jordan

Time: 5 hours 15 minutes to 8 hours

Distance to trailhead: 26.2 miles

Water Availability: Plenty along West Fork Yankee Fork; Lightning Creek; several side streams

Cautionary Advice: *Trail passes through burn area. Bring sun protection. The first two crossings of Lightning Creek can be a challenge in early season. Although the hike has an elevation range of only 700 feet, the many ups and downs add up to a total gain of 1900 feet.*

Additional Information: Salmon-Challis National Forest, Challis-Yankee Fork Ranger District (208) 879-4100

Coordinates

Trailhead:

North 44d22.234
West 114d44.700

End of trail:

North 44d25.343
West 114d47.398

West Fork of Yankee Creek/Lightning Creek

The first part of the trail leads through sagebrush hillsides before it enters burn area. The Potato Fire in 2006 burned more than 18,000 acres and some of the area along the West Fork of Yankee Creek. Although stark with the many burned snags, the wildflowers add a nice contrast.

At 3.4 miles, the Lightning Creek trail turns north up a narrow canyon. The terrain is rugged and few venture into these woods. Solitude is almost guaranteed. The final destination is a scenic setting next to the creek.

Trailhead Directions

From Stanley, drive north on Highway 75 for 12.8 miles. Turn left at the Sunbeam Village onto the paved Yankee Fork Road. The pavement ends at 3.0 miles and changes to gravel. Follow the good gravel road another 4.8 miles and turn left on forest road 074 into the ghost town of Bonanza.

Road 074 will pass by the Forest Service guard station and Boot Hill Cemetery and arrive at the West Fork Trailhead 1.0 mile from the turnoff. Restrooms are available.

The Hike

The trail begins along an old dirt road that is usually gated. Follow the road down into the canyon through sagebrush. At 0.2 miles the road splits; stay to the right. Pass a gravel pit and the single-path trail begins at 0.4 miles.

The trail leads through sagebrush before entering forest. The West Fork of Yankee Creek glistens below to the left of the trail. Soon the trail enters a burn area.

The trail now climbs 350 feet up a ridge to avoid a steep gorge along the creek. The trail reaches the top of the knoll at 1.2 miles with views to the west of the appropriately named Red Mountain (9,387 feet).

Descend along switchbacks back down to the valley floor. Continue hiking through burn area, passing below interesting rock formations at 1.9 miles. Arrive at a signed junction at 2.0 miles where the Deadwood Creek Trail departs to the left. Continue along the West Fork of Yankee Creek.

Reenter forest at 2.5 miles and then skirt the edge of a talus slope. The trail now enters a large meadow, turns north and arrives at another signed junction at 3.4 miles. Turn right towards Lightning Creek through a field of wildflowers.

At 3.6 miles cross Lightning Creek. Although not usually a problem, this ford can be challenging in early season. A few downed trees assist with the crossing. Go through forest with the canyon narrowing before crossing the creek again at 4.1 miles.

After crossing the creek, the trail begins a steep climb through two switchbacks. The trail now heads up the canyon, remaining 200 to 300 feet above Lightning Creek. At 5.3 miles, the trail drops almost 100 feet into a side canyon with a tributary stream. After crossing the stream, the trail rises about 200 feet and then traverses along the steep slope again. After topping out at a little over 7,200 feet, the trail makes a gradual decline to the base of Lightning Creek at 6.5 miles. The dense forest makes for an ideal lunch spot along the translucent creek.

This is the end of the hike. Continuing north on the trail, just over another 4.5 miles, eventually leads to Lightning Lake.

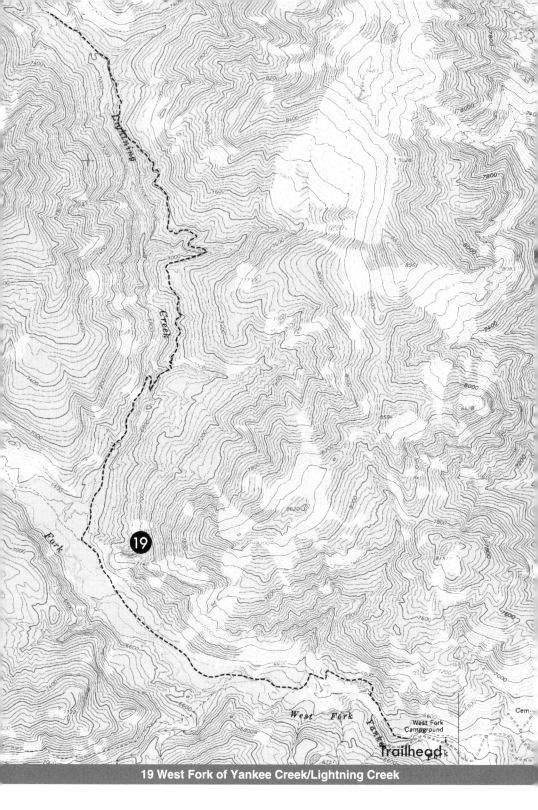

19 West Fork of Yankee Creek/Lightning Creek

N

Rough Lake

Distance: 9.4 miles roundtrip

Total elevation gain: 1950 feet

Difficulty: Difficult

Elevation Range: 7400 feet to 9100 feet

Topographic Map: Casino Lakes

Time: 4 hours to 6 hours 15 minutes

Distance to trailhead: 13.5 miles

Water Availability: Plenty along Rough Creek and Rough Lake

Cautionary Advice: *Rough Lake is a little less than 1/2 mile off trail. Off trail skills and the Casino Lakes quad are highly recommended.*

Additional Information: Sawtooth National Recreation Area (208) 774-3000

Coordinates
Trailhead:

North 44d13.332
West 114d47.254

Rough Lake:

North 44d10.945
West 114d47.928

Rough Lake

Rough Lake sits just below an unnamed peak at 9,654 feet. Dense forest surrounds the shallow lake. Solitude is almost guaranteed at this exquisite destination. The trail, embellished with wildflowers, wanders along translucent Rough Creek up to the lake. After crossing Rough Creek at the 2.4 mile mark, the trail begins a steep climb with fine views of the surrounding landscape.

Trailhead Directions

From Stanley, drive 9.4 miles on Highway 75 and turn right over a bridge that crosses the Salmon River. A sign indicates Rough Creek. Follow the well-graded dirt road, forest road 626, for 2.2 miles. Here the road makes a hard left. Do not take the right or center fork. Instead stay left and follow the road an additional 1.9 miles to its end at the trailhead.

The Hike

Sign in at the trailhead register and begin the hike on level ground. Numerous varieties of wildflowers grow along this trail in early and midsummer. Hike through dense forest and cross a small steam at 0.3 miles. At 0.5 miles, cross crystal clear Rough Creek on downed logs. The trail now meanders through forest and then makes a gradual ascent along Rough Creek. At 2.4 miles, cross Rough Creek. Stay alert, because there have been numerous sightings of black bears in this area.

Get ready for some exercise — the trail's grade steepens once across Rough Creek. At 2.7 miles, make the first switchback. A fairly worn trail goes straight at this switchback; do not take this trail because it descends back down to the creek. Continue to climb as views improve. Come to a clearing at 3.0 miles as the trail's grade flattens. Go another 0.2 miles to a signed junction. The left fork leads to Lookout Mountain in 2.6 miles (Hike 21).

Turn right at the fork towards Garland Lake. The trail now leads through a lovely stretch of forest along the southeast edge of the canyon. At 4.2 miles, the trail intersects with another trail that leads to Lookout Mountain. Reach a flat saddle just beyond the trail intersection.

From the saddle, Rough Lake is about 0.4 miles off trail. To find Rough Lake, leave the trail and hike northwest (right) up the hillside to about 9,150 feet. Turn right, or north, at this elevation and go through the forest until the lake becomes visible below. From here, scramble down the hillside to the south shore of the lake.

Trailhead

Creek

Creek

Creek

Rough
Lake

21

20

Lookout

20 ROUGH LAKE / 21 LOOKOUT MOUNTAIN

N

21 Lookout Mountain

Distance: 11.6 miles roundtrip

Total elevation gain: 2650 feet

Difficulty: Very difficult

Elevation Range: 7350 feet to 9950

Topographic Map: Casino Lakes

Time: 5 hours 15 minutes to 7 hours 45 minutes

Distance to trailhead: 13.5 miles

Water Availability: Plenty along Rough Creek. No reliable water past the last crossing of Rough Creek.

Cautionary Advice: *This hike can be deceiving because much of the elevation gain happens in the last 3 1/2 miles. You need to be in good physical condition to reach the top. Watch for possible thunderstorm activity because Lookout Mountain is dangerous when lightning threatens.*

Additional Information: Sawtooth National Recreation Area (208) 774-3000

Coordinates
Trailhead:

North 44d13.322
West 114d47.254

Lookout Mountain:

North 44d11.556
West 114d45.518

Lookout Mountain

Unrivaled views, a crystal-clear creek, wonderfully dense forests and a trail off the beaten path reward those who take this hike. Wildflowers shoulder the trail the first 2 miles of the hike. Over the next 3.8 miles, you will travel through beautiful rugged country—but it is almost straight up for a gain of over 2,100 feet. The final destination is Lookout Mountain.

The views from this perch are almost indescribable. Lookout Mountain lies in the northeast corner of the White Clouds at an elevation of 9,954 feet. The Warm Springs Creek drainage separates this peak by over 4 miles from the main group of White Cloud Peaks. Standing on top of Lookout Mountain feels like you're on an island in the sky.

Dramatic vistas include the White Clouds, the Sawtooths, the Salmon River Mountains and the Lost River Range. No camera can capture the beauty of these vistas.

Dramatic vista north from Lookout Mountain.

Trailhead Directions

From Stanley, drive 9.4 miles on Highway 75 and turn right over a bridge that crosses the Salmon River (there will be a sign indicating Rough Creek). Follow the well-graded dirt road, forest road 626, for 2.2 miles. At this point the road will make a hard left. Do not take the right or center fork. Follow the road an additional 1.9 miles to its end at the trailhead.

The Hike

The hike begins on level ground. Hike through dense forest and cross a small steam at 0.3 miles. At 0.5 miles, cross Rough Creek on downed logs. The trail now winds its way through forest and then makes a gradual ascent along Rough Creek. At 2.4 miles, cross Rough Creek. Stay alert, because there have been numerous sightings of black bears in this area.

Get ready for some serious exercise because once across Rough Creek, the trail's grade steepens. At 2.7 miles, make the first switchback. Views improve as you continue to climb. At 3 miles, come to a clearing as the trail's grade flattens. Go another 0.2 miles to a signed junction. The right fork leads to Rough Lake (Hike 20). Take the left fork to Lookout Mountain. The sign indicates it is 2 miles, but from this junction it is closer to 2.6 miles to the summit.

Begin climbing again through forest to another junction with a large granite outcrop at 3.9 miles. The right fork runs parallel with the earlier trail off to the right to Rough Lake and eventually leads past Rough Lake and to the Garland Lakes. Go down the left fork and walk east along the ridgeline. Enjoy the outstanding views of the drainages and surrounding mountains to the north and south.

After crossing the ridge at 4.7 miles, the grade steepens. The trail is quite scenic with the many whitebark pines and boulders shouldering the trail. After a set of 15 breath-challenging switchbacks the trail ends at the top of Lookout Mountain.

 **Little Casino Creek**

Distance: 9.0 miles roundtrip

Total elevation gain: 1250 feet

Difficulty: Moderate

Elevation Range: 6150 feet to 7300 feet

Topographic Map: East Basin Creek, Casino Lakes, Stanley

Time: 3 hours 45 minutes to 5 hours 30 minutes

Distance to trailhead: 5.8 miles

Water Availability: Readily available along Little Casino Creek

Cautionary Advice: *Get an early start. Because of low elevation, trail may be hot by midday in the summer. Bring sun protection, because the lower portion of the trail is in partial forest.*

Additional Information: Sawtooth National Recreation Area (208) 774-3000

Coordinates

Trailhead:

North 44d15.136
West 114d51.529

Meadow:

North 44d12.096
West 114d53.237

Little Casino Creek

The Little Casino Creek trail is a wonderful hike in a narrow canyon. Many wildflower-filled meadows and old mining ruins enhance the trail. Interesting rock outcrops on the upper portion of the trail invite off-trail exploration. The final destination offers a very pleasant meadow with views of Thompson Peak (10,761 feet), the highest mountain in the Sawtooths.

Trailhead Directions

Drive north on Highway 75 for 5.3 miles. Turn right and cross a bridge over the Salmon River on forest road 651. Follow the well-graded forest road 0.5 miles to the road's end and a large parking area.

The Hike

From the trailhead parking area, head southwest to the trailhead that begins as an old Jeep road. Fortunately, the road is short lived and at 0.2 miles the trail becomes a single path and crosses the creek. Continue on the west side of the creek through sagebrush and partial forest.

At 0.6 miles, the trail enters a narrow meadow along the creek. You'll find many excellent spots for picnics with children. The canyon begins to narrow at 1.0 mile and soon passes an old mining site on the right. Cross the creek again at 1.5 miles. The trail now meanders through a couple of small meadows. At 2.1 miles, the trail runs along the edge of one final meadow, turns right through the meadow, and crosses over the creek again on logs.

Once across the creek, the canyon begins to narrow again as the trail gains elevation through lodgepole forest. Very interesting rock outcroppings appear on the right at 2.8 miles. If time permits, these jagged formations invite further exploration.

The trail flattens and begins the first of six crossings of the creek at 3.2 miles. After the last crossing, the trail's grade steepens again. Over the next 1/2 mile, the trail stays close to the small creek wandering through lodgepole forest. At 4.1 miles, the canyon opens with views of the sagebrush hillsides. The trail arrives at the north end of the meadow at 4.5 miles. Hills on the far side of the meadow perfectly frame Thompson Peak.

For an impressive view of the Sawtooths, continue along the edge of the meadow for about 100 feet. Look to the right for a faint trail leading up the open hillside. This trail becomes more prominent after a few minutes of hiking and after a 0.3 mile hike and 250 feet of gain, arrives at a knoll with marvelous views of the Sawtooth Mountains.

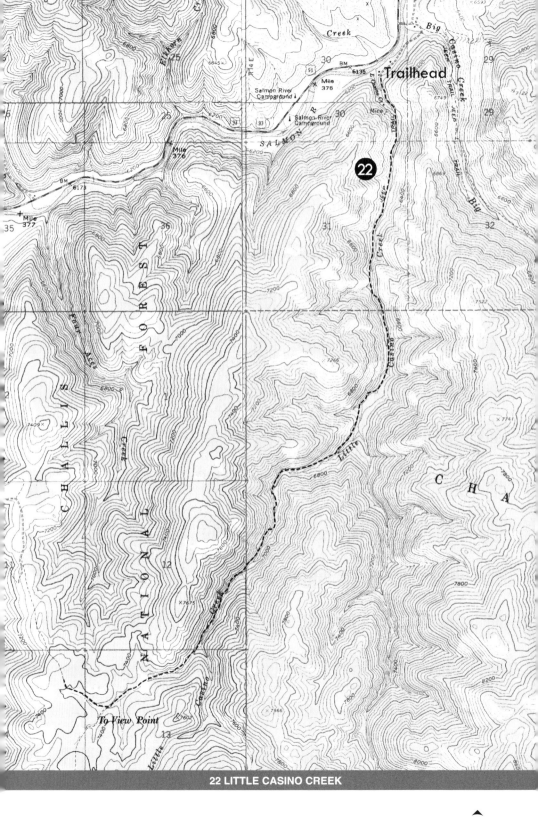

Trailhead

N

Big Casino Creek

Distance: 12.6 miles roundtrip

Total elevation gain: 2450 feet

Difficulty: Very difficult

Elevation Range: 6150 feet to 8600 feet

Topographic Map: East Basin Creek, Casino Lakes

Time: 5 hours 30 minutes to 8 hours 15 minutes

Water Availability: Plenty along Big Casino Creek, Lower Casino Lake

Cautionary Advice: *In summer get an early start as the low elevation can make the trail hot by midday. Bring sun protection for the sun exposure on the lower portion of the partially forested trail.*

Distance to trailhead: 5.5 miles

Further Information: Sawtooth National Recreation Area (208) 774-1116

Coordinates

Trailhead:

North 44d15.342
West 114d51.309

Lower Casino Lake:

North 44d10.701
West 114d49.125

Big Casino Creek

Lodgepole forest and marsh grass surround the lower Casino Lake, and another lake awaits just over 1/4 of a mile beyond the lower lake. A wonderful talus slope on the east side of the lake enhances its beauty and wildflowers add color to the scenery. The trail to the lakes begins in sparse forest with sagebrush and aspen covered hillsides. Further along the hike, the canyon narrows and the forest becomes dense, adding to the allure. Few people hike this trail, so solitude may be an added perk. In early fall, aspen give the first 2 miles of trail added color.

Trailhead Directions

Drive north on Highway 75 for 5.3 miles. Turn right and cross a bridge over the Salmon River on forest road 651. Follow the well-graded forest road 0.2 miles to the trailhead parking area on the left.

The Hike

Just beyond the trail register, the trail crosses Big Casino Creek. Keeping your boots dry can be a challenge depending on water flow. Although not particularly deep, the crossing's water flow depth can get to about mid-calf. Once across the creek, the trail follows an old road for a short distance. After crossing the creek, another old road leads off to the left. Stay right at this junction. At 0.3 miles, the trail crosses the creek again on a downed tree. In early summer, the valley floor contains a variety of lush vegetation.

From the valley floor, opposing hillsides create a nice contrast. On the east: sagebrush covers the hill. On the west: a lodgepole forest. At 0.8 miles, the trail crosses the creek again and then into an open hillside. The trail soon turns southwest and passes some interesting rock outcrops at 1.2 miles. With a little imagination, the interesting rock shapes may conjure up images of creatures. Just beyond this area, the trail flattens out along the creek and makes a good turnaround spot for those hiking with children.

The canyon begins to narrow at 1.6 miles with patches of aspens on the hillsides. Cross Midwinter Creek at 2.2 miles. Once across the creek, the trails grade steepens. The grade intensifies in a thin lodgepole grove. At 3.4 miles the trail skirts a moraine (glacially formed accumulation of unconsolidated glacial debris) and then enters dense forest. The dark forest and steep canyon walls add a cozy seclusion.

Continue gaining elevation and making various crossings of Big Casino Creek and various side streams. The trail's grade finally begins to flatten at 5.9 miles and crosses the outlet of the lower Casino Lake. Once across the outlet, the trail crosses a side stream and reaches the lower Casino Lake at 6.3 miles.

The second of the three Casino Lakes can be reached by continuing along the main trail another 0.3 miles and 200 feet of elevation gain.

Trailhead

23

N

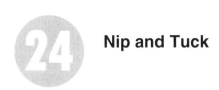

Nip and Tuck

Distance: 2.0 mile roundtrip

Total elevation gain: 600 feet

Difficulty: Easy

Elevation Range: 6300 feet to 6900 feet

Topographic Map: Stanley

Time: 45 minutes to 1 hour 30 minutes

Distance to trailhead: 1.8 miles

Water Availability: Nip and Tuck Creek across road from parking area and along first section of trail along unnamed creek

Cautionary Advice: *Most of this hike is exposed, so bring plenty of sun protection. The majority of the hike is off-trail so route finding skills are helpful, although due to the open terrain it is easy to recognize your location.*

Additional Information: Salmon-Challis National Forest, Challis-Yankee Fork Ranger District (208) 879-4100

Coordinates

Trailhead:

North 44d14.086
West 114d55.796

Viewpoint:

North 44d14.439
West 114d55.616

Nip and Tuck

Once the snow has disappeared in the foothills, this is an excellent short hike. The trail, if you can call it that, leads north just short of a 1/2 mile along an unnamed creek. From here, it is another 1/2 mile of nontechnical scrambling up a scenic canyon to a ridge. The panoramic vistas from this location are simply stunning. Views include a good portion of the Sawtooths, the Stanley Basin and Sawtooth Valley, and extend almost to the Galena Summit some 40 miles away, the White Clouds, and the Salmon River Mountains.

Trailhead Directions

Drive north on Highway 75 for 1.3 miles to Lower Stanley. Turn left on an unmarked dirt road (forest road 633). From the highway turnoff, drive 0.5 miles to a parking area on the right. You won't find a sign at the trailhead, so use your odometer when you turn off of Highway 75 to find the trailhead.

The Hike

The hike begins on the unmarked trail along a small stream that channels into Nip and Tuck Creek. In the summer, cattle are sometimes grazing in this area. The trail runs along the unnamed creek through sagebrush for 0.4 miles. At this point, look to the right for a drainage leading up the ridge.

Hike up the steep drainage. The easiest route is just to the right of the drainage bottom, making sure to avoid any rocky portions with exposed drop-offs. Midway up the hillside, interesting shaped rock outcroppings appear on the open hillsides. After 0.5 miles and a little more than 400 feet of gain, approach a saddle. From the top of the saddle, turn right or south towards the hilltop about 500 feet away. Have a snack and observe the stellar views of the valley below, the Sawtooths, and the other surrounding mountains.

For a better view of the Salmon River along Highway 75, head another 0.15 miles to the southwest to another hilltop.

If you have the time, the ridge area is an interesting place to explore.

Retrace your steps back to the trailhead.

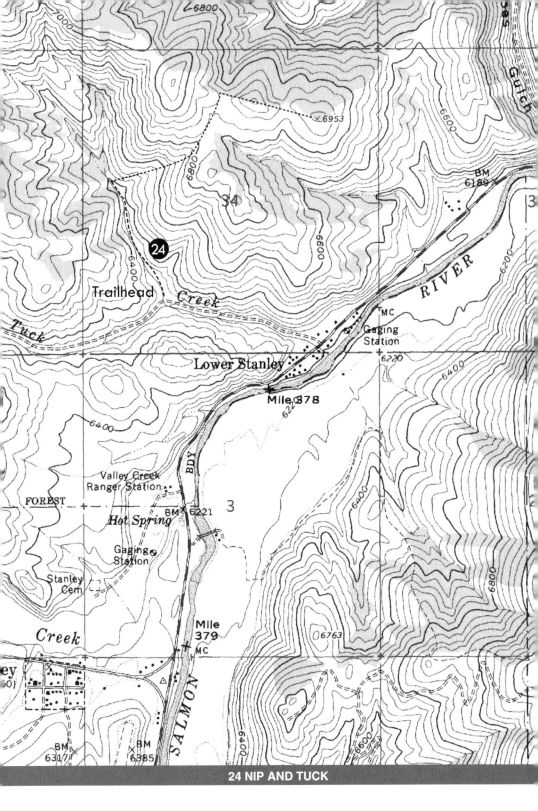

N

Boundary Creek to the Sunny Gulch Trail

Distance: 8.0 miles to saddle

Total elevation gain: 2750 feet

Difficulty: Difficult

Elevation Range: 6800 feet to 9550 feet

Topographic Map: Casino Lakes

Time: 4.0 hours to 6.0 hours

Distance to trailhead: 6.4 miles

Water Availability: Bring water. There is a creek crossing at 0.4 mile but after that there is no reliable water.

Cautionary Advice: *Get an early start. The trail's southern exposure can make it very hot in the middle of summer. Bring sun protection for the open hillsides on the upper part of the trail. You will find reliable water at the first creek crossing 0.4 miles from the trailhead, but that's it. Watch for thunderstorm activity near the saddle.*

Further Information: Sawtooth National Recreation Area (208) 774-3000

Coordinates

Trailhead:

North 44d09.404
West 114d52.062

Saddle on Boundary Creek Trail:

North 44d10.080
West 114d49.509

Boundary Creek to the Sunny Gulch Trail

The lung-busting, steep Boundary Creek Trail climbs straight up until you reach the saddle. The views make this hike worth every step. The first 2 miles include outstanding over-the-shoulder vistas of the Sawtooth Range, Sawtooth Valley, and a new perspective of the famous Redfish Lake.

Once at the saddle, take in the breathtaking views. Just below the ridge, the largest and highest Casino Lake glistens. To the west beyond the Sawtooth Valley: The serrated peaks of the Sawtooths dance across the skyline. To the north: the rugged Salmon River Mountains. To the east and south: the White Clouds where Castle Peak (11,815 feet) dominates the horizon.

In the fall, the aspen on the first 1.5 miles of the trail add color.

Redfish Lake from the Boundary Creek trail.

Trailhead Directions

Drive south 5.6 miles from Stanley on Highway 75. Turn left onto the well-graded forest road 212, also known as Boundary Creek Road, and drive 0.8 miles to the road's end.

The Hike

The trail begins from the parking area with a gradual ascent through a sagebrush meadow. At 0.25 miles, enter forest of lodgepole pine, Douglas fir and aspen. After 0.4 miles and 200 feet of gain cross a small bridge over Boundary Creek. After crossing the bridge, a small footpath heads down to Boundary Creek, an excellent spot for a picnic with children. If you are hiking with children, do not hike beyond this point. The steep and strenuous grade may inspire a mutiny.

After crossing the bridge, the trail's grade steepens and begins heading north. At 0.6 miles, the first of many switchbacks improves the views across the valley and to the Sawtooths. In fall, the aspens display brilliant red, yellow and orange hues. At 0.9 miles, enter an open hillside and at 1.1 miles, reenter the forest. Notice a huge, old-growth Douglas fir on the right with an impressive six-foot diameter.

Continue climbing and at 1.6 miles make a switchback to head north.

Just beyond the switchback on the left, a small knoll provides outstanding views of Redfish Lake, the Sawtooth skyline and the Sawtooth Valley below.

At 1.8 miles, make the first of two more switchbacks. For the next mile there are very few trees for shade. Across the valley, Mt. Heyburn (10,229 feet), Horstman Peak (10,470), Thompson Peak (10,761) and Williams Peak (10,635) rise impressively to the sky.

The trail turns left (east) at 2.2 miles. Get ready for a workout. The trail's grade intensifies and follows an open hillside to a signed junction.

From the junction, turn right on the Sunny Gulch trail towards the Casino Lakes. The trail enters forest and gains 280 feet in 0.5 miles to the ridge's crest with a scenic meadow beyond. The trail skirts the meadow on the left and then rises steeply again at 3.5 miles. Views of the Salmon Mountains soon appear and at 3.8 miles, the aqua-colored upper Casino Lake can be seen below. Continue to the top of the saddle at 4.0 miles at an elevation of 9,550 feet. Wander around this splendid spot to take in the expansive views of the Sawtooths, the White Clouds, and the Salmon River Mountains.

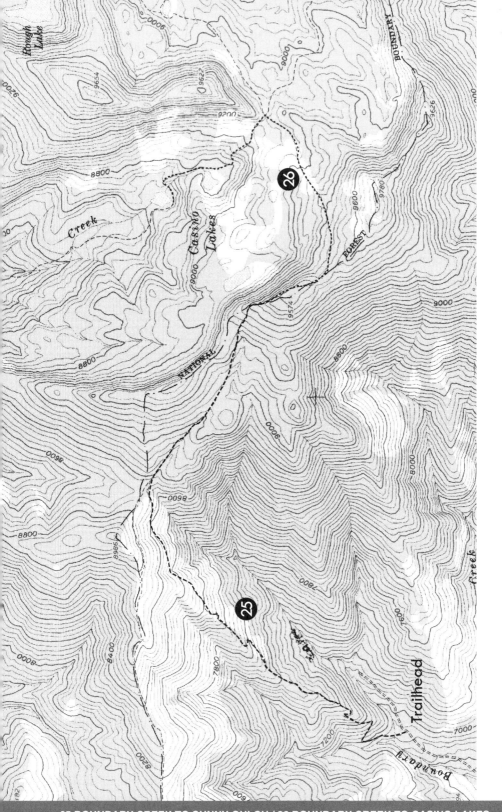

Boundary Creek to the Casino Lakes

Distance: 11.4 miles roundtrip to second Casino Lake

Total elevation gain: 3650 feet

Difficulty: Very difficult

Elevation Range: 6800 feet to 9550 feet

Topographic Map: Casino Lakes

Time: 5 hours 45 minutes to 8 hours 30 minutes

Distance to trailhead: 6.4 miles

Water Availability: One creek crossing near the trailhead, several streams past the saddle and the Casino Lakes

Cautionary Advice: *Get an early start. The trail's southern exposure can make it very hot in the middle of summer. Bring sun protection for the open hillsides on the upper section of trail. More than any other hike in the book, this hike gains the most elevation so you must be in excellent physical condition to complete this hike. Be aware of thunderstorm activity near the saddle.*

Further Information: Sawtooth National Recreation Area (208) 774-3000

Coordinates
Trailhead:

North 44d09.404
West 114d52.062

2nd Casino Lake:

North 44d10.549
West 114d49.000

Boundary Creek to the Casino Lakes

Bird's eye views along the Boundary Creek trail reveal the Sawtooth Valley, Redfish Lake and an inspiring look at the Eastern Face of the Sawtooths. Beyond the saddle, the trail descends to a splendid meadow filled with wildflowers.

The final destination is a visit to two of the three Casino Lakes. Marsh grass surrounds the first lake and a granite talus ridge borders the south side of the more-scenic lower lake.

Trailhead Directions

Drive south 5.6 miles from Stanley on Highway 75. Turn left onto the well-graded forest road 212, also known as Boundary Creek Road, and drive 0.8 miles to the road's end.

The lowest of the Casino Lakes.

The Hike

Follow hike 25 along Boundary Creek Trail to the saddle.

From the saddle, the trail descends through forest and scenic rock formations. Within a 1/2 mile, enter a very scenic meadow. The meadow contains many wildflowers including lupine, penstomen, yarrow and indian paintbrush. At 4.8 miles, cross a small stream that is not shown on the Casino Lakes 7.5 topo map. This stream is the first reliable water source since crossing the bridged stream near the trailhead. Continue another 0.2 miles to a signed junction. From the saddle (where this hike started), the descent to the junction is close to 400 feet. Remember on the return, this section will be a steep ascent.

At the signed junction, turn left towards the Casino Lakes. The trail descends steeply, a 300-foot elevation loss, through lodgepole forest dropping to the first Casino Lake (8,800 feet) in 0.4 miles. To visit the lower and more scenic of the two Casino Lakes, continue down another 0.3 of a mile and a 160 foot elevation loss. Remember, to get back to the car from the lower Casino Lake, it is 5.7 miles and almost 900 feet of gain back to the saddle and then down to the trailhead. This is a very demanding hike.

Fourth of July Lake and Washington Lake

Distance: 5.6 miles roundtrip

Total elevation gain: 1000 feet

Difficulty: Moderate

Elevation Range: 8750 feet to 9550 feet

Topographic Map: Boulder Chain Lakes, Washington Peak

Time: 2 hours 30 minutes to 3 hours 45 minutes

Distance to trailhead: 24.4 miles

Water Availability: Plenty along Fourth of July Creek and Lake and Washington Lake; several side streams

Cautionary Advice: *This trail is heavily used. Avoid weekends. To avoid residual snow in the high elevation, begin the hike after mid-to late July.*

Additional Information: Sawtooth National Recreation Area (208) 774-3000

Coordinates

Trailhead:

North 44d02.791
West 114d39.456

Washington Lake:

North 44d01.902
West 114d37.413

Fourth of July Lake and Washington Lake

Flanked by several small meadows that teem with wildflowers by mid-to late July, shallow Fourth of July Lake sits in the middle of a U-shaped bowl. Numerous 10,000-foot plus mountains can be seen from the lakes' shore with the majestic Patterson Peak (10,872 feet) stealing the show.

One mile further, along with a 240 foot climb and a 200 foot descent, lies the much larger and deeper Washington Lake. Sheer cliff walls rise up 1,000 feet from the lake's north shore. A couple of small meadows with wildflowers provide additional scenery.

Trailhead Directions

From Stanley, drive south on Highway 75 for 14.5 miles. Turn left onto the Fourth of July Creek Road, forest road 209. Follow this road 9.9 miles to the large parking area on the right. Restrooms are available at the trailhead.

Fourth Of July Lake

The Hike

The trailhead sign states that Fourth of July Lake and Washington Lake are 1 1/4 miles and 2 miles respectively. The actual distance is closer to 1.8 and 2.8 miles. The Washington Peak 7.5 quad is inaccurate. The initial part of the trail has been rerouted from what is shown on the map.

The trail begins by crossing a bridge over the Fourth of July Creek and then crosses the Jeep road to Phyllis Lake. Enter dense forest at 0.5 miles and then cross two creeks on downed logs. Cross another stream at 0.9 miles before the trails grade steepens. At 1.5 miles the trail flattens with outstanding views to the north.

Reach a signed junction at 1.6 miles. The left fork leads over the ridge top and down into Ants Basin. Go straight or east another 500 feet to Fourth of July Lake. In season, various wildflowers including bistort, sego lily, shooting star, valerian, and aster bloom in the surrounding meadows.

To reach Washington Lake, cross the outlet creek, and go up the ridge. Reach the crest at 2.3 miles and see picturesque views of the surrounding peaks. The trail now drops down 200 feet to the southwestern edge of beautiful Washington Lake.

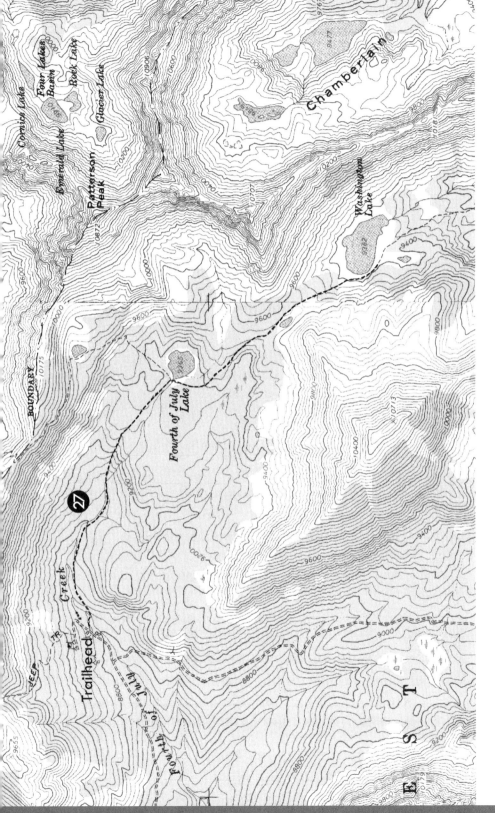

Corniee Lake
Four Lakes Basin
Rock Lake
Emerald Lake
Glacier Lake
Patterson Peak
Chamberlain
Washington Lake
BOUNDARY
Fourth of July Lake
Creek
TR
JEEP
Trailhead
Fourth of July
EST

27

N

28 Horton Peak

Distance: 6.8 miles roundtrip

Total elevation gain: 2750 feet

Difficulty: Difficult

Elevation Range: 7150 feet to 9900

Topographic Map: Alturas Lake, Horton Peak

Time: 3 hours 45 minutes to 5 hours 30 minutes

Distance to trailhead: 20.6 miles

Water Availability: NONE

Cautionary Advice: *NO WATER. The first few miles of trail are shouldered with sagebrush, so wear long pants to protect lower legs from getting scratched. The first 1.5 miles has very few trees, so protect yourself from sun exposure.*

Additional Information: Sawtooth National Recreation Area (208) 774-3000

Coordinates

Trailhead:

North 43d57.435
West 114d46.904

Horton Peak Lookout:

North 43d57.942
West 114d44.904

Horton Peak

The view from Horton Peak across to the Sawtooth ridgeline is astounding. Panoramic views include the Sawtooths, the White Clouds, and the Boulder and Pioneer Mountains. Rugged mountains can be seen from every direction.

This is a good hike for early summer when the wildflowers bloom and the Sawtooths still sleep under a blanket of snow. Fall is another outstanding time to hike because of the aspens near and along the trail.

Remember, reliable water is not available on the trail. For the first 1.5 miles, trees are few and far between. The trail rises straight up to the top on more than 35 switchbacks that offer very few flat sections.

Trailhead Directions

From Stanley, drive 15.1 miles South on Highway 75 and turn left onto gravel Valley Creek Road just past Champion Creek. For 4.5 miles, passing many spur dirt roads on the left and right, follow this forest road 194 to a dirt road on your left that marked with a sign, "Horton Peak Lookout 3." Turn left and follow this dirt road 1 mile to the end.

The Hike

The trail begins in sagebrush and a few solitary aspen. The first of three switchbacks arrives at 0.1 miles. At 0.3 miles, the trail heads north and reaches a wonderful rock formation on the right with a few scattered trees. If you have small children, or are out for a short jaunt, this is a wonderful perch to admire the valley below and the Sawtooth skyline.

The trail continues north and at 0.7 miles begins another set of three switchbacks. At 0.8 miles, the trail heads north again and wildflowers begin to intermingle with the sagebrush. Two more switchbacks and the trail arrives at the first turnaround spot. The views are impressive with various rock outcroppings and a few trees adding additional scenery. In the fall, this site offers spendid views of colorful aspen.

Continue hiking through more switchbacks and finally enter forest at 1.4 miles. At 1.7 miles cross a knoll to find another great spot for a picnic with good tree cover, interesting rock formations, wonderful views of the Sawtooth mountains and a nice aspen grove.

From here, the trail leads through an aspen grove before heading out into the sagebrush again. Views to Alturas Lake across the expansive Stanley Basin are marvelous. Continue through four switchbacks and at 2.6 miles, the trail turns north with a neck-bending view up to the top of Horton Peak. From here, eight more switchbacks and 0.8 miles take you to the top. Near the top, several of the switchbacks taunt with glimpses of the White Clouds.

Views from the summit are exceptional! To your west: the Salmon River meanders through the Sawtooth Valley backed by Alturas, Pettit and Yellow Belly lakes that sit in the foreground of the imposing Sawtooth skyline. Look to the northeast for the White Clouds to rise up in all of their majestic beauty with Castle Peak (11,815 ft.) above all the others. To the southeast: the dramatic Boulder Mountains with five named peaks over 11,000 feet, including Galena Peak (11,153 ft.) less than 9 miles away.

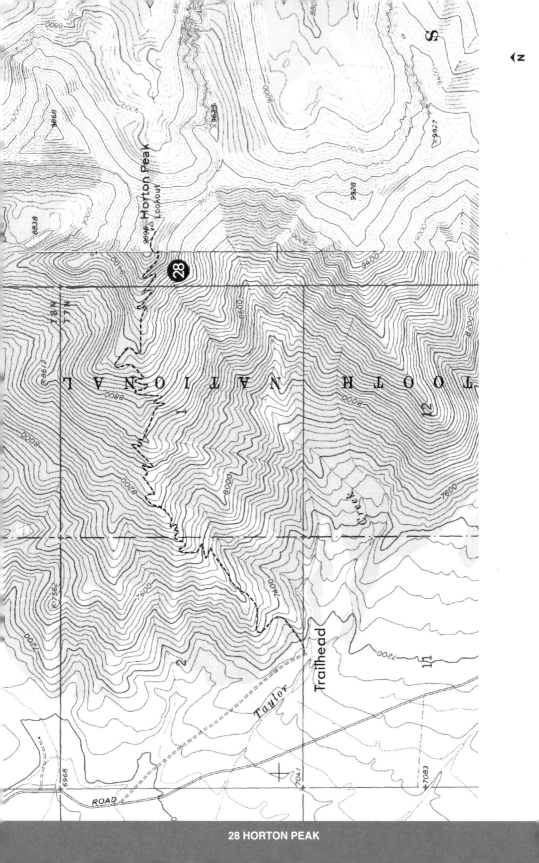

 # Alpine Creek

Distance: 6.2 miles roundtrip

Total elevation gain: 550 feet

Difficulty: Easy

Elevation Range: 7050 feet to 7550

Topographic Map: Snowyside Peak

Time: 2 hours 15 minutes to 3 hours 30 minutes

Distance to trailhead: 26.5 miles

Water Availability: Alpine Creek

Cautionary Advice: *Trail passes through many open areas. Bring sun protection.*

Further Information: Sawtooth National Recreation Area (208) 774-3000

Coordinates

Trailhead:

North 43d53.880
West 114d54.219

End of trail:

North 43d54.306
West 114d57.175

Alpine Creek

The hike along Alpine Creek offers stunning beauty. To the north of the trail, steep granite walls rise over 2,000 feet. The path leads in and out of scenic meadows that in season become awash with buckwheat, monkshood, lupine, agoseris, and fireweed. The last 1.5 miles of the trail has many granite benches offering exquisite picnic sites. In early fall, several meadows with aspen stands make a colorful hike.

Trailhead Directions

Drive south from Stanley on Highway 75 for 20.5 miles. Turn right onto Alturas Lake Road #205. Follow this road for 5.0 miles past Alturas Lake. Here the road turns to gravel and in another 1.5 mile the road ends at the trailhead. There is ample parking and restrooms.

Granite walls to the north along the Alpine Creek Trail.

The Hike

From the large parking area, head west on the main trail along Alturas Lake Creek. At 0.1 mile find a signed junction. Turn right and begin a relatively flat hike through lodgepole pine and Douglas-fir forest. Soon the trail's grade steepens and at 0.8 mile arrives at the wilderness boundary. Obtain your wilderness permit here. At 1.0 mile, the trail enters a small clearing with a patch of aspen, returns to forest and then breaks out into a small meadow.

On the left, a granite knoll (7,486 feet) with a faint footpath leads to the top with superb views. The knoll makes a good final destination with small children. The backside of the knoll is quite steep, so keep little ones within arm's length.

From the knoll, the trail continues through sagebrush and then enters a small segment of tree cover. At 1.2 miles, the trail breaks out into another meadow with sagebrush, wildflowers and small groves of aspen. The trail returns to forest after a 1/4 mile and Alpine Creek is just 100 feet off to the left. From here, the trail alternates between meadow and tree cover before arriving alongside the creek at 1.9 miles.

The trail now stays in close proximity to the translucent creek. Along this stretch, there are plenty of spots for a break and to admire the outstanding scenery. At 2.6 miles, the trail ascends on a series of granite slabs. It then enters forest that leads out into a final meadow just below the granite walls leading up to an unnamed peak (10,269 feet).

The trail ends in a lovely stand of forest with several footpaths down to the creek.

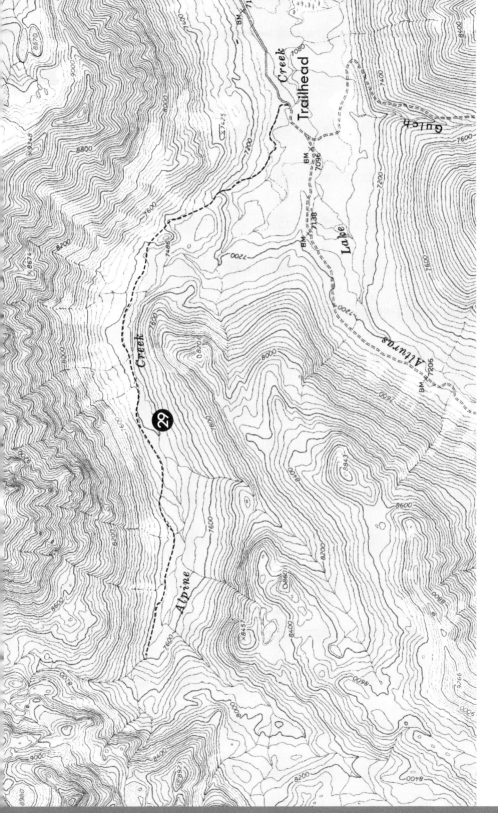

Eureka Gulch

Distance: 8.0 miles roundtrip

Total Elevation gain: 1700 feet

Difficulty: Difficult

Elevation Range: 7050 feet to 8750 feet

Topographic Map: Snowyside Peak, Marshall Peak

Time: 3 hours 30 minutes to 5 hours 15 minutes

Distance to trailhead: 26.5 miles

Water Availability: Plenty along Alturas Lake Creek and Eureka Gulch Creek

Cautionary Advice: *In early season, crossing the creek from Eureka Gulch at 0.9 miles make it challenging to keep your boots dry so bring a pair of sandals or tennis shoes. The last mile of trail is very rocky, so wear a good pair of hiking boots.*

Additional Information: Sawtooth National Recreation Area (208) 774-3000

Coordinates

Trailhead coordinates:

North 43d53.879
West 114d54.217

Ruby Mine:

North 43d52.106
West 114d54.039

Eureka Gulch

Abundant wildflowers, incredible views of many unnamed ridges in the Smoky Mountains and a visit to an old mine reward those willing to hike the 1,700 foot gain to the mine. Not much is left of the mine these days except for a few rusty scraps of metal and a collapsed tunnel into the hillside. The views from the old mine are phenomenal.

Although most of this trail was an old Jeep road, Mother Nature and the forest service have done an excellent restoration job. Much of the road is not apparent anymore and the trail is quickly converting to a single footpath.

Trailhead Direction

Drive south from Stanley on Highway 75 for 20.5 miles. Turn right onto Alturas Lake Road #205. Take this road for 5.0 miles past Alturas Lake.

Open hillside along Eureka Gulch.

Here the road turns to gravel. Follow to the road's end in another mile. Find ample parking and a restroom.

The Hike

Find the trailhead and begin hiking at the northwest edge of the parking area. Arrive at a signed junction with the trail to Alpine Creek (Hike 29). Continue straight. At 0.5 miles, cross a bridge over Alpine Lake Creek and then come to another junction at 0.7 miles. Turn left here towards Eureka Gulch. The trail meanders along the valley floor through sparse forest with plenty of wildflowers. At 0.9 miles, cross the creek that drains Eureka Gulch. Early-season hikers should bring a pair of sandals to cross this creek. If there is standing water after crossing the creek, you can avoid the water by staying to the right and walking through the forest. After crossing the creek, the trail emerges into an open area, crosses a smaller stream at 1.3 miles and ambles through forest.

After going through this area, the trail's grade changes from level to steep and regresses back to the Jeep road. The going is steep, but fortunately dense forest protects against the sun. After 1.8 miles and a 450-foot gain, the trail takes a short break from the incline. Catch your breath — at 1.9 miles, the incline begins again. At 2.1 miles, the trail breaks out into the open with views into the Smoky Mountains and an over-the-shoulder look at the rocky peaks of Alpine Creek Canyon. From here, the trail gains elevation and emerges into open areas and back into forest. Views of the open hillside meadows are beautiful.

At 2.8 miles, the trail's grade becomes very steep and rocky. Soon the trail breaks out into a wonderful basin with a large open hillside on the left. The trail flattens at 3.1 miles and leaves the creek. Here the trail makes a switchback and starts a long traverse across the hillside. At 3.6 miles, the trail comes to another switchback and a road leads off to the left. DO NOT TAKE THIS ROAD. Instead, switchback again across the ridge and come to a fork at 3.9 miles. Go left and up the fork about 150 yards to the site of the old Ruby Mine. The tunnel into the hillside has collapsed but you can clearly see where it entered the mountain.

The views are divine from this perch. Looking north you'll see the serrated pinnacles of the mountains in the Alpine Creek Canyon. To the south and west are the many unnamed 9,000-foot-plus peaks of the Smoky Mountains.

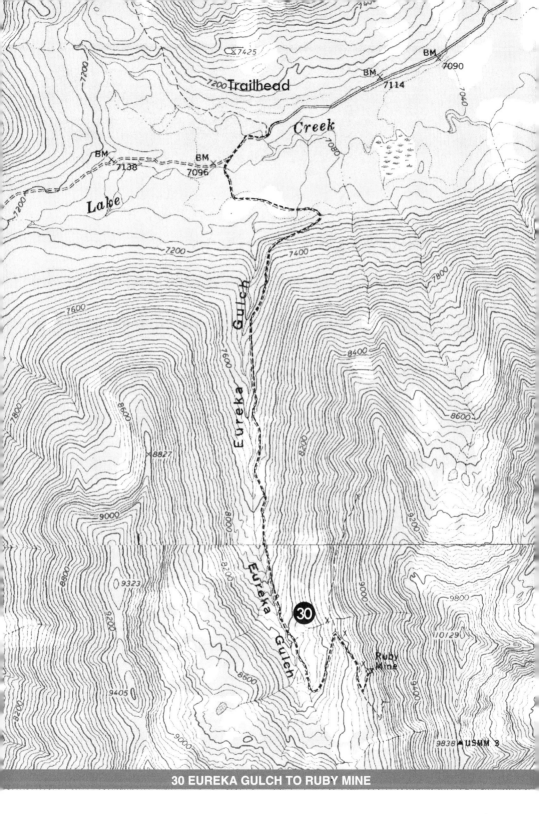

Cabin Creek Lakes

Distance: 7.6 miles roundtrip

Total elevation gain: 2000 feet

Difficulty: Difficult

Elevation Range: 7100 feet to 9100 feet

Topographic Map: Snowyside Peak, Alturas Lake

Time: 3 hours 30 minutes to 5 hours 15 minutes

Distance to trailhead: 24.2 miles

Water Availability: Plenty along Cabin Creek and Cabin Creek Lakes

Cautionary Advice: *The Snowyside Peak circa 1964 quad does not show the trail. This is not an issue as the trail is maintained to the lake at 8811 feet.*

Further Information: Sawtooth National Recreation Area (208) 774-1116

Coordinates

Trailhead:

North 43d56.227
West 114d51.295

1st Cabin Creek Lake

North 43d55.039
West 114d54.388

2nd Cabin Creek Lake:

North 43d55.202
West 114d54.437

Cabin Creek Lakes

This maintained trail ends at the Cabin Lakes' basin. Because the trail does not continue deeper into the Sawtooths, traffic tends to be lighter than many other trails in the Alturas Lake area. This hike entices with wonderful views, seasonal wildflowers, two pristine mountain lakes, and off-trail explorations. It's definitely a steep hike, but worth every step.

Trailhead Direction

From Stanley, head south on Highway 75 for 20.5 miles. Turn right on paved Alturas Lake Road. Drive 2.7 miles and turn right on the the gravel road 207. Look for the "Cabin Creek Organization Camp" sign. Drive 0.8 miles and turn left at the sign "Cabin Creek Trail." Drive another 0.2 miles to the road's end and the Cabin Creek Trailhead.

The Hike

The trail begins between a sagebrush-covered hill and the scenic Cabin Creek. In season, lupine is scattered among the sagebrush and showcases a beautiful contrast. Within 0.2 miles, arrive at the trail register. Get your wilderness permit and head west along Cabin Creek.

Trees along the creek's edge provide shade as the trail gains elevation. The open, sagebrush-covered hillsides are filled with a variety of wildflowers, including indian paintbrush, larkspur, buckwheat, bistort, sego lily, groundsel and many others. At 0.7 miles, leave the creek; the trail veers left into an open meadow.

The trail heads up the north side of Cabin Creek Canyon and in and out of forests of stately Douglas fir trees. At 1.8 miles, the trail approaches an open hillside and visits the creek again. This is a nice turnaround for those with small children. In season, the arrow-shaped leaves and the yellow flowers of the arrowleaf balsamroot along with other flowers paint the hillside. At 2.7 miles, you'll officially enter the Sawtooth Wilderness.

From the wilderness boundary, the trail crosses a stream and then rises steeply 600 feet up to the lake in 0.8 miles. This section of trail may be a physical challenge, but it's quite scenic. A beautiful granite wall drops into the northwest side of the lake that sits at 8811 feet.

To reach the highest Cabin Lake, follow the trail along the east side of the lower lake. At the end of the lake, a faint trail will head northwest up a steep gully. At the top of the ridge, turn left towards the outlet stream. You will have hiked another 0.3 miles and gained another 270 feet.

The upper Cabin Lake lies at 9078 feet and is enclosed in a beautiful semi-cirque. Take the time, if you have it, to explore the wonderful topography.

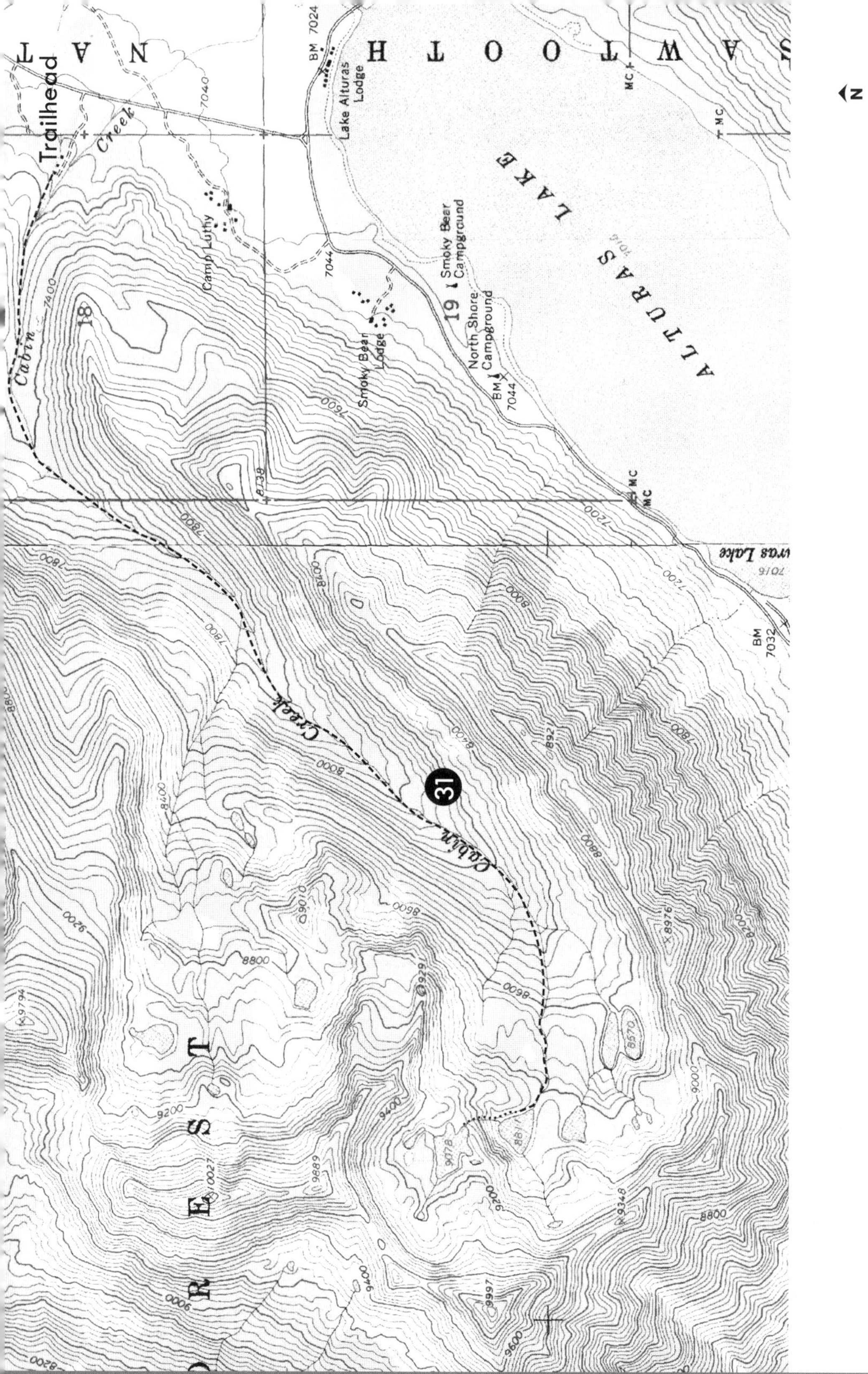

N

SAWTOOTH

NATIONAL

FOREST

Trailhead

Cabin Creek

Camp Lutty

Camp Perkins

Lake Alturas Lodge

BM 7024

7040

7040

7044

Smoky Bear Lodge

18

19

North Shore Campground

Smoky Bear Campground

BM 7044

ALTURAS LAKE

Alturas Lake

7016

BM 7032

Cabin Creek

31

 **Alice Lake**

Distance: 11.4 miles roundtrip

Total elevation gain: 1600 feet

Difficulty: Difficult

Elevation Range: 7000 feet to 8600 feet

Topographic Map: Alturas Lake, Snowyside Peak

Time: 4 hours 30 minutes to 7 hours

Distance to trailhead: 19.8 miles

Water Availability: Pettit Lake, creeks, ponds and Alice Lake

Cautionary Advice: *Early season hikers may find the many stream crossings difficult due to high water. Hikers should be prepared to wade. The crossings may even be impassable in very high runoff years. Because the upper portions of the trail are exposed to the sun, be prepared with hat, sunglasses and sunscreen.*

Information: Sawtooth National Recreation Area (208) 774-3000

Coordinates

Trailhead:

North 43d59.052
West 114d52.332

Alice Lake:

North 43d56.604
West 114d56.506

Alice Lake

Alice Lake lies at the end of a glaciated bowl. Numerous peaks, including the heavenly granite monolith El Capitan (9,901feet) and the stately Snowyside Peak (10,651 feet) surround this amazing lake. Wildflowers adorn many portions of the trail. Within the first mile, look for a scenic display of arrowleaf balsamroot. The upper section of the trail includes penstomen, columbine, cinquefoil, indian paintbrush, pussytoes, monkshood and many others. This trail gets plenty of use but traffic tends to fall off the further into the wilderness you go. Just before the 2 mile mark, families can find a great turnaround point along the creek that offers a pleasant little waterfall.

Trailhead Directions

Drive 17.7 miles south from Stanley on Highway 75 and turn right on

Meadow, Sawtooth Valley and the distant White Cloud Peaks.

gravel Pettit Lake Road. A sign indicates "Pettit Lake." Follow this road 1.5 miles to a four-way intersection. Turn right, cross the bridge, stay to your left at the "Y" intersection and drive 0.6 miles to the Tin Cup Transfer Camp parking area. Find the trailhead at the southwest corner of the parking area. Restrooms are available.

The Hike

The trail starts out in sagebrush and comes to a signed junction at 0.2 mile. The right-hand trail leads over a ridge and drops down to another junction with options for Yellow Belly Lake (Hike 33) or to Farley/Toxaway Lakes (Hike 34/35). Take the left fork towards Alice Lake. The trail skirts the north shore of Pettit Lake with a sagebrush covered hillside on the right. In early summer, the very beautiful arrowleaf balsamroot wildflower grows profusely. Continue along the trail through Douglas fir and lodgepole pine to the Sawtooth Wilderness boundary at 1.2 miles. Get your wilderness permit here.

The trail now meanders through dense forest and will soon reveal impressive views of the imposing granite walls below Parks Peak (10,280 feet). Continue past a granite rockslide and at 1.9 miles, the trail will come within a few yards of the creek that drains out of Alice Lake. If you have children, a pleasant waterfall makes for an excellent picnic spot and turnaround.

The trail continues to gain elevation with the first creek crossing at 2.3 miles. In early season, the crossing may be impassable.

Once across the creek, the trail continues through forest and breaks out into a lovely stand of aspen at 2.8 miles. Ford the creek again on downed logs. At 3.0 miles, the trail exits forest into a huge meadow and begins five switchbacks up an exposed slope. In season, this area is usually covered with a large array of wildflowers.

The views continue to improve as the trail crosses below the magnificent granite walls of Parks Peak. The aspen in this area enhance early fall hiking. Cross a small side stream and then reenter forest area at 3.5 miles.

From here the trail makes two quick switchbacks, goes through granite talus, and snakes through four more switchbacks at 4.0 miles. In the next 1/2 mile, make two creek crossings on downed logs and then a final ascent of 6 switchbacks.

A well-built bridge spans the creek at 4.8 miles. Photography buffs will want to take advantage of the jaw-dropping views of the drainage

El Capitan behind Alice Lake.

below, the Stanley Basin, and the pointed tips of the White Clouds that seize the horizon.

The trail levels out after meandering through beautiful woods and making one final creek crossing at 5.3 miles. Beyond the creek crossing, the trail arrives at two picturesque ponds. The wildflower display in the meadows here is quite phenomenal. Continue past the ponds and arrive at the northeast side of Alice Lake (8,596 feet).

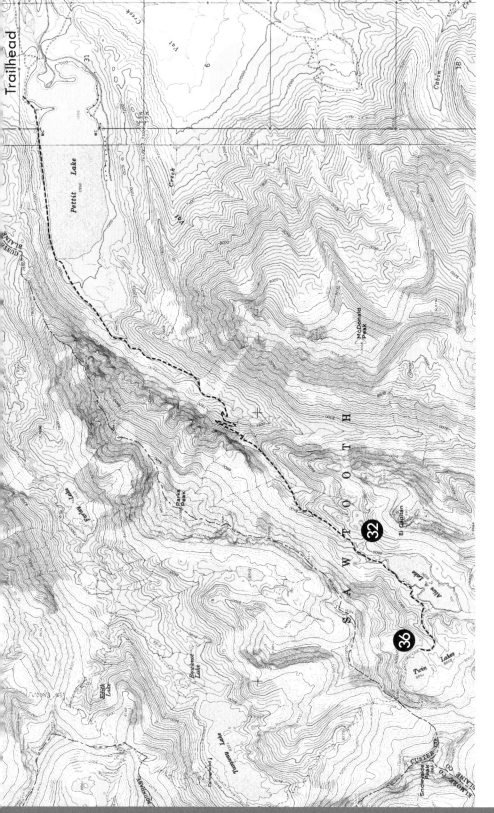

Yellow Belly Lake

Distance: 4.8 miles roundtrip

Total elevation gain: 1000 feet

Difficulty: Moderate

Elevation Range: 7000 feet to 7500 feet

Topographic Map: Alturas Lake, Snowyside Peak

Time: 2 hours 15 minutes to 4 hours 15 minutes

Distance to trailhead: 19.8 miles

Water Availability: Pettit Lake, Yellow Belly Lake, small pond on top of ridge above Pettit Lake

Cautionary Advice: *None*

Additional information: Sawtooth National Recreation Area (208) 774-3000

Coordinates
Trailhead:

North 43d59.052
West 114d52.332

Yellow Belly Lake:

North 43d59.839
West 114d52.744

Yellow Belly Lake

This is a good hike for early season hikers. The trail's highest point is just over 7,500 feet, reducing your odds of running into snow. Families with small children will find the 0.9 mile one-way hike to the ridge challenging because of the 500 feet of gain, but it is certainly doable.

The views from the ridge of Parks Peak (10,208 feet), McDonald Peak (10,068 feet), Pettit Lake, and the canyon leading to Alice Lake are delightful. The final destination is heavily forested, 188-acre Yellow Belly Lake. The shore of the lake is sandy and the clear water makes for good swimming in the heat of summer.

Trailhead Directions

Drive 17.7 miles south from Stanley on Highway 75 and turn right on gravel Pettit Lake Road. A sign indicates "Pettit Lake." Follow this road

View from ridge above Pettit Lake.

1.5 miles to a four-way intersection. Turn right, cross the bridge, stay to your left at the "Y" intersection and drive 0.6 miles to the Tin Cup Transfer Camp parking area. Find the trailhead at the southwest corner of the parking area. Restrooms are available.

The Hike

Begin the hike at the Tin Cup trailhead located in the southwest corner of the parking area. The trail begins in sagebrush and quickly comes to a signed junction. The left fork leads to Alice Lake (Hike 32). Take the right fork towards Yellow Belly Lake.

The trail begins a gradual traverse along a hillside interspersed with sagebrush and trees. At 0.4 miles, the views of the surrounding mountains include McDonald Peak (10,068 feet) to the south and Parks Peak (10,280 feet) to the west. Wonderful views of the drainage from Alice Lake are highlighted at 0.6 miles.

After climbing a little over 500 feet from the trailhead, the trail flattens at 0.9 miles. A small pond off to the left is a good spot for a turnaround if you are with small children.

The trail stays level across the ridge and at 1.1 miles begins descending to Toxaway Canyon. Notice how dense the forest becomes on the north side of the ridge compared to the sun-exposed south side. After descending 400 feet, arrive at a signed junction 1.9 miles from the trailhead.

Turn right and proceed about 100 feet to another junction with a trail on the left leading to McDonald Lake. The lake is shallow and marshy and is only 0.3 miles away. Continue 0.4 miles along the main trail through woods. Here the trail will intersect with a Jeep road. Turn left and walk 0.1 miles to Yellow Belly Lake (7,076 feet) for a total of 2.4 miles from the trailhead. The road dead ends into the lake and is a charming spot to swim or have a picnic. To explore this area, head back to the trail/road junction and turn left along the south shore of the lake.

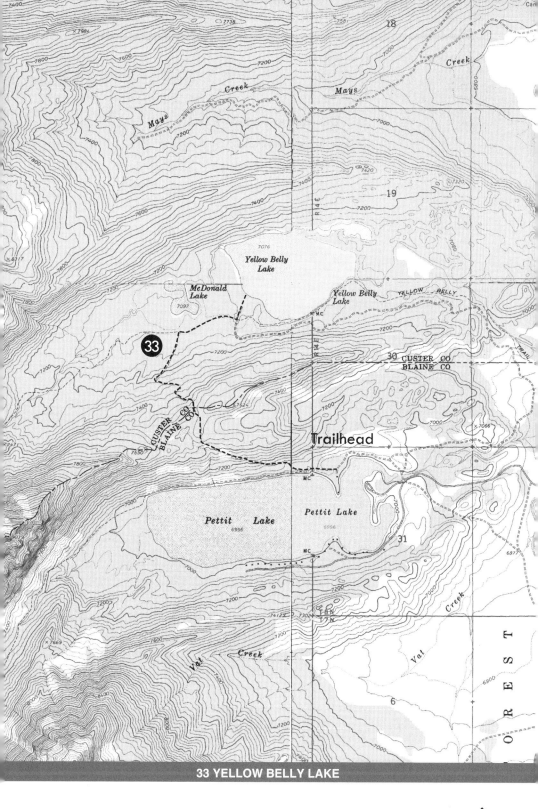

N

 **Farley Lake**

Distance: 9.4 miles roundtrip

Total elevation gain: 1600 feet

Difficulty: Difficult

Elevation Range: 7000 feet to 7750 feet

Topographic Map: Alturas Lake, Snowyside Peak

Time: 3 hours 45 minutes to 6 hours

Distance to trailhead: 19.8 miles

Water Availability: Plenty along outlet of Farley Lake and Farley Lake; small pond on top of ridge above Pettit Lake

Cautionary Advice: *Difficult creek crossing that may be impassable in early season.*

Additional information: Sawtooth National Recreation Area (208) 774-3000

Coordinates

Trailhead:

North 43d59.052
West 114d52.332

Farley Lake:

North 43d58.867
West 114d55.799

Farley Lake

Picturesque Farley Lake lies nestled between the towering Imogene (10,125 feet) and Parks Peaks (10,208 feet). Cliffs from Parks Peak tumble into the south side of the lake and enhance the lake's beauty. The trail to Farley Lake is also quite exquisite. After crossing the moraine from Pettit Lake, the trail descends into Toxaway Canyon. Heading west into the canyon leads through forest and a myriad of wonderful talus slopes, flower-filled meadows, waterfalls, and streams.

Trailhead Directions

Drive 17.7 miles south from Stanley on Highway 75 and turn right on the gravel Pettit Lake Road. Look for the "Pettit Lake" sign. Follow this road 1.5 miles to a four-way intersection. Turn right, cross the bridge, stay to your left at the "Y" intersection, and drive 0.6 miles to the Tin

Cup Transfer Camp parking area. There are restrooms in the parking area.

The Hike

Begin the hike at the Tin Cup trailhead. The trail starts in sagebrush and quickly comes to a signed junction. Here, the left fork leads to Alice Lake (Hike 32). Take the right fork toward Yellow Belly Lake. The trail begins a gradual traverse along a hillside peppered with sagebrush and trees. At 0.4 miles, views of the surrounding mountains, including McDonald Peak (10,068 feet) to the south and Parks Peak (10,280 feet) to the west, continue to improve. Wonderful views of the drainage into Alice Lake are highlighted at 0.6 miles.

After climbing a little more than 500 feet from the trailhead, the trail flattens at 0.9 miles. To the left is a small pond, which is a good turnaround spot for those with children.

The trail stays level across the ridge and at 1.1 miles lowers to Toxaway Canyon. Notice how dense the forest becomes on the north side of the ridge compared to the sun-exposed south side. After descending 400 feet, arrive at a signed junction 1.9 miles from the trailhead.

Turn left at the junction towards Toxaway and Farley lakes. The Sawtooth Wilderness boundary is within 500 feet. From here the trail remains relatively flat until a creek crossing at 2.9 miles. This creek is the drainage for the canyon and in early season will be difficult or impossible to cross.

Once across the creek, pass a small meadow on the right and at 3.1 miles begin climbing through two switchbacks. Good views of the White Clouds appear on the left after the second switchback. The trail flattens at 3.4 miles and then skirts the edge of a talus slope at 3.8 miles.

Continue a gradual climb until the trail breaks out of the forest and into a meadow at 4.2 miles. This pleasant meadow is stunning with its backdrop of granite walls below Imogene and a cascading waterfall on the south side of the trail. Beyond the meadow, the trail gains about 200 feet along a granite hillside. From this perch, on a clear day, the White Clouds, including Castle Peak (11,815 feet) make a majestic view. At 4.7 miles, arrive at Farley Lake (7,745 feet). Continue hiking west along the trail to locate several footpaths leading down to the lake.

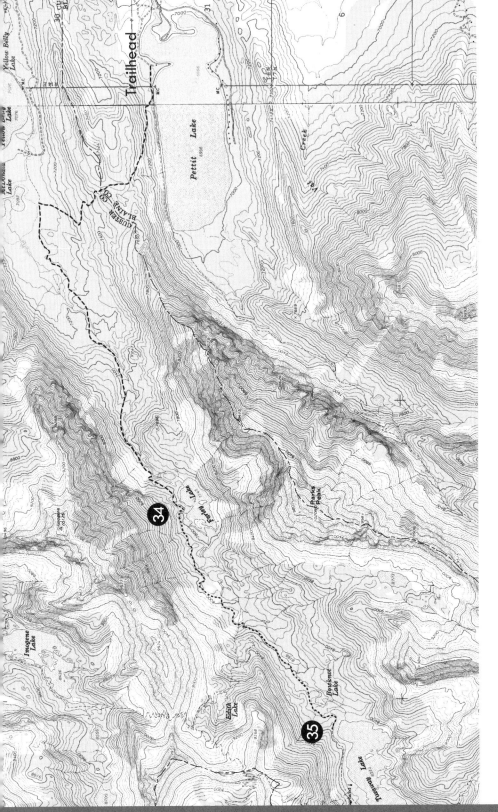

Toxaway Lake

Distance: 14.6 miles roundtrip

Total elevation gain: 2100 feet

Difficulty: Difficult

Elevation Range: 7000 feet to 8250 feet

Topographic Map: Alturas Lake, Snowyside Peak

Time: 6 hours to 9 hours

Distance to trailhead: 19.8 miles

Water Availability: Toxaway Lake, Farley Lake, Pettit Lake, several streams

Cautionary Advice: *Difficult creek crossing. Bring sun protection for the exposed hillsides.*

Additional information: Sawtooth National Recreation Area (208) 774-3000

Coordinates

Trailhead:

North 43d59.052
West 114d52.332

Toxaway Lake:

North 43d57.80
West 114d57.60

Toxaway Lake

The trail to Toxaway Lake is a wonderful trek. From the ridge above Pettit Lake the path descends into Toxaway Canyon. Heading west into the canyon, the trail passes a myriad of wonderful talus slopes, flower-filled meadows, waterfalls, and many streams.

Next comes scenic Farley Lake, which is nestled between the towering Imogene (10,125 feet) and Parks peaks (10,208 feet). From here, the trail gains another 600 feet in 2.6 miles to reach the northeast shore of Toxaway Lake. Toxaway is a massive glacial lake at just over a mile long. Snowyside Peak (10,651 feet) and another unnamed granite beauty (10,052 feet) offer wonderful vistas beyond the lake.

Trailhead Directions

Drive 17.7 miles south from Stanley on Highway 75 and turn right on gravel

Toxaway Lake and the Sawtooth Mountains.

Pettit Lake Road. A sign indicates "Pettit Lake." Follow this road 1.5 miles to a four-way intersection. Turn right and cross the bridge. Stay to the left at the "Y" intersection and drive 0.6 miles to the Tin Cup Transfer Camp parking area. Restrooms are available.

The Hike

Follow Hike 34 to Farley Lake. The trail stays high as you leave the northeast portion of Farley Lake. Aspen and subalpine fir are scattered amongst sagebrush. At 5.0 miles, pass a spring-fed pool just to the left of the trail.

The trail now leaves Farley Lake and meanders through sagebrush. At 5.5 miles, a 30-foot-plus lovely waterfall cascades off to the left just before crossing a small stream and entering forest.

At 6.0 miles, the trail arrives at a spectacular talus slope just below an unnamed peak (9,934 feet). To the left of the trail a flower-filled meadow creates a striking contrast to the stark talus slope. Various sized granite benches appear at 6.2 miles, offering excellent spots to enjoy a snack.

Come to a signed junction at 6.4 miles. For a nice side excursion, follow the right fork up to Edith Lake, which has 1.0 mile and 450 feet of gain. Continue west towards Toxaway Lake. Pass a small, unnamed lake (8,165 feet) at 6.6 miles.

Just beyond the small lake, at 6.8 miles, look to the left. Just a few yards off the trail, the creek flows over granite flats and creates an exquisite little waterfall. The trail now crosses a platform bridge over a tiny stream that flows into a small pond. Reach Bowknot Lake at 7.0 miles. Just beyond the lake cross another stream and arrive at Toxaway Lake at 7.3 miles.

Twin Lakes

Distance: 13.6 miles roundtrip

Total elevation gain: 2150 feet

Difficulty: Very difficult

Elevation Range: 7000 feet

Topographic Map: Alturas Lake, Snowyside Peak

Time: 6 hours 15 minutes to 11 hours

Distance to trailhead: 19.8 miles

Water Availability: Plentiful throughout hike

Cautionary Advice: *Early season hikers may find the many high-water stream crossings difficult. The crossings may be impassable in very high runoff years. Be prepared to wade. The upper portions of the trail are exposed to the sun so be prepared with hat, sunglasses and sunscreen.*

Additional Information: Sawtooth National Forest (208) 774-3000

Coordinates

Trailhead:

North 43d59.052
West 114d52.332

Alice Lake:

North 43d56.343
West 114d57.274

Twin Lakes

By hiking another 1.1 miles from Alice Lake, high-octane hikers can add Twin Lakes to their itinerary. These two pristine lakes, set just below Snowyside Peak (10,651 feet) and many other unnamed peaks, create a divine background. The two lakes are divided by an isthmus of stunted trees, granite outcroppings and fallen timber. Mountain heather and other wildflowers add to the beauty of these two mountain gems.

Trailhead Directions

Drive 17.7 miles south from Stanley on Highway 75 and turn right on gravel Pettit Lake Road. A sign indicates "Pettit Lake." Follow this road 1.5 miles to a four-way intersection. Turn right, cross the bridge, stay to your left at the "Y" intersection, and drive 0.6 miles to the Tin Cup Transfer Camp parking area. Restrooms are available.

The Hike

Follow Hike 32 to Alice Lake. To reach Twin Lakes from the northeastern edge of Alice Lake, follow the trail southwest along the edge of the lake. Camera buffs will be challenged to keep moving because of the cornucopia of outstanding scenery. At 0.2 miles the trail leaves the lake and the grade eventually steepens. Pass by a small pond at 0.5 miles and then begin the first of three switchbacks before crossing a talus slope.

Just beyond the talus slope, outstanding views of beautiful Alice Lake appear. At 1.0 miles, arrive at a signed junction, not shown on the Snowyside 7.5 quad. The right trail goes up and over Snowyside pass and then descends to Toxaway Lake. Turn left and descend 100 feet to the lakes.

One of the Twin Lakes and the Sawtooth Mountains.

Hell Roaring Creek Pond

Distance: 2.6 miles roundtrip

Total elevation gain: 350 feet

Difficulty: Easy

Elevation Range: 6800 to 7150 feet

Topographic Map: Mt. Cramer, Obsidian

Time: 1 hour to 1 hour 30 minutes

Distance to trailhead: 15.5 miles

Water Availability: Plenty along Hell Roaring Creek

Cautionary Advice: *In early season, Hell Roaring Creek may be a raging torrent. Keep a close eye on children around the creek.*

Additional Information: Stanley Ranger Station (208) 774-3000

Coordinates

Trailhead:

North 44d01.541
West 114d50.518

West end of the pond:

North 44d01.835
West 114d51.923

Hell Roaring Creek Pond

If you're short on time or looking for an easy excursion, this is a pleasant hike. Children may also find this trail entertaining. For a good part of the hike, Hell Roaring Creek tumbles loudly. Wonderful views from the foothills, reveal the White Clouds and Stanley Basin. At the end of the hike, a wonderful little pond with many boulders creates a natural playground.

Trailhead Direction

From Stanley, drive south on Highway 75 for 14.5 miles. Turn right onto the Decker Flat Road #210. Drive 0.2 miles over the Salmon River and turn left. The trailhead parking is 0.3 miles on the right past the trailhead. The parking area has room for four or five cars, so if the area is full, park in the large parking area to the left of the Salmon River bridge.

The Hike

The hike begins in sagebrush before climbing south up a hill. Views of the Stanley Basin and the foothills of the White Clouds improve with each step. The trail briefly overlooks the creek, turns north through woods and at 0.4 miles begins running parallel with Hell Roaring Creek. At 0.8 miles, the trail flattens out and the roar of Hell Roaring Creek subdues. At 1.0 miles, the translucent creek and the trail come within a few feet of each other offering places to sit under a lodgepole pine and watch the creek meander by.

The pond is 20 to 30 yards off of the trail and is hidden by a natural bunker, so it can be a little challenging to find. Continue along the trail another 0.25 miles and break out into an area where the forest is not as dense and black and tan boulders are scattered among the lodgepoles. Look right, to the north, where the bunker flattens. Turn right off of the trail and just beyond the bunker find the western edge of the pond. Walk around to the east shore of the pond for top-notch views of the Sawtooth skyline rising beyond Hell Roaring Lake.

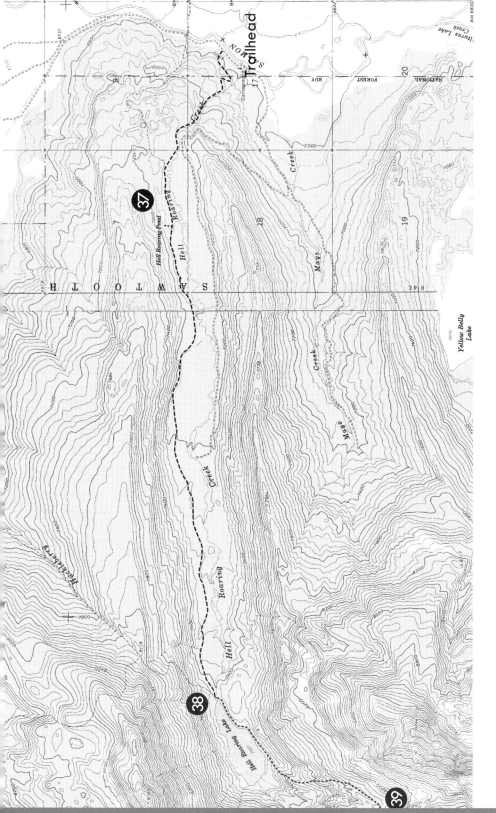

Hell Roaring Lake

Distance: 10.0 miles roundtrip

Total elevation gain: 600 feet

Difficulty: Moderate

Elevation Range: 6800 feet to 7200 feet

Topographic Map: Mt. Cramer, Obsidian

Time: 3 hours 45 minutes to 5 hours 30 minutes

Distance to trailhead: 15.5 miles

Water Availability: Along Hell Roaring Creek and at Hell Roaring Lake

Cautionary Advice: *No water after 2.1 miles on the trail until you reach the lake.*

Additional Information: Sawtooth National Recreation Area (208) 774-3000

Coordinates

Trailhead:

North 44d01.541
West 114d50.518

Hell Roaring Lake:

North 44d01.601
West 114d55.716

Hell Roaring Lake

A walk in the woods, this hike is one of the flattest hikes in the book. Most of the elevation gain occurs during the first and the last mile of the hike. Views of the Sawtooths do not open up until just before arriving at the lake. But oh, what views!

Just beyond the majestic Hell Roaring Lake are the imposing granite walls of the Sawtooths. In the far distance, Mt. Cramer (10,716 feet), the second-highest peak in the Sawtooths, and Sevy Peak (10,272 feet) cloud the horizon. Closer to the lake, The Finger of Fate, rises up almost 800 vertical feet. This tower of solid granite is one of the most technically challenging rock climbing routes in the Sawtooths. Other granite sculptures near the Finger of Fate include The Arrowhead, The Coffin, The Birthday Cake, The Sentry and The Red Bluff.

Hell Roaring Lake and the distant Finger of Fate.

Trailhead Direction

From Stanley, drive 14.5 miles south on Highway 75. Turn right onto the Decker Flat Road #210. Drive 0.2 miles over the Salmon River and turn left. The trailhead parking is 0.3 miles on the right, past the trailhead. The parking area has room for four or five cars, so if the area is full, park in the large parking area to the left of the Salmon River bridge.

The Hike

Follow hike 37. After leaving the pond, the main trail meanders through a delightful young lodgepole forest. At 2.1 miles from the trailhead, the trail and Hell Roaring Creek come together again. This is the last time the creek is visible from the trail until arriving at the lake, so this is a good place to fill up your water bottles. Continue along the flat trail and at 3.2 miles arrive at the wilderness boundary. Obtain your wilderness permit here.

From the wilderness boundary, the trail ascends through forest that adds subalpine fir and Douglas fir to the lodgepole trees. Arrive at a signed junction five miles from the trailhead. Turn left toward Imogene Lake and cross the outlet stream of Hell Roaring Lake on a small bridge. The views are marvelous.

Hell Roaring Lake to View

Distance: 13.5 miles roundtrip

Total elevation gain: 1200 feet

Difficulty: Difficult

Elevation Range: 6800 feet 8000 feet

Topographic Map: Obsidian, Mt. Cramer

Time: 5 hours to 7 hours 45 minutes

Distance to trailhead: 15.5 miles

Water Availability: Along Hell Roaring Creek and at Hell Roaring Lake, several stream crossings above Hell Roaring Lake

Cautionary Advice: *No water after 2.1 miles on the trail until reaching the lake.*

Additional Information: Sawtooth National Forest (208) 774-3000

Coordinates
Trailhead:

North 44d01.541
West 114d50.518

View Site:

North 44d00.938
West 114d56.342

Hell Roaring Lake to View

This hike takes in Hell Roaring Pond and then ventures on to spectacular Hell Roaring Lake. The trail skirts the southern shoreline of the lake and then gains elevation through wonderful forest. The scenery of the granite walls, ridges and peaks are breathtaking. The elevation gain improves the view and offers a stellar bird's eye perspective of Hell Roaring Lake.

Trailhead Direction

From Stanley, drive south 14.5 miles on Highway 75. Turn right onto Decker Flat Road #210. Drive 0.2 mile over the Salmon River and turn left. The trailhead parking is 0.3 mile on the right past the trailhead. There is room here for four or five cars and if you find it full, you will need to park back at the large parking area to the left of the Salmon River bridge.

The Hike

Follow hike 36 and 37. Once across the bridge over the outlet creek over Hell Roaring Lake, the trail heads southwest along the lake's shoreline. At 0.3 miles, cross a small unnamed stream on boulders and at 0.5 miles cross a bridge over another unmarked stream. Here the trail's grade steepens and soon makes the first of four switchbacks. After the first switchback, look for a gorgeous view down to the lake and across to the myriad of granite peaks.

For the best views, continue hiking beyond the switchbacks through a small gully and then complete two more switchbacks. The trail was rerouted from what is shown on the Mt. Cramer topo map and consequently does not show any of the switchbacks.

Cross a bridge over a boggy area at 1.4 miles and then make one last switchback. From here, the trail heads across an open hillside with small lodgepoles on the left.

Views off to the right are spectacular on this stretch. The trail will soon make a 90° turn and a few yards past this bend is the termination of this hike. There is nothing spectacular to indicate that you are at this point other than the incredible view. From here, the scenery is heavenly. If you find yourself entering dense forest on both sides of the trail and the views have disappeared, you have gone too far and need to turn around.

Lily Lake and Redfish Lake Creek Falls

Distance: 1.4 miles (To Redfish Lake Creek Falls)

Total elevation gain: 250 feet

Difficulty: Easy

Elevation Range: 6550 feet to 6800

Topographic Map: Mt. Cramer

Time: 45 minutes to 1 hour. This time does not include the boat ride to and from Redfish Inlet.

Distance to trailhead: 5.9 miles

Water Availability: Redfish Lake, Lily Pad Lake, creeks and streams

Cautionary Advice: *The slopes above the falls can be slippery. Keep children close.*

Additional Information: Sawtooth National Recreation Area (208) 774-1116

Coordinates
Trailhead (Redfish Inlet):

North 44d06.005
West 114d57.169

Redfish Lake Creek Falls:

North 44d05.769
West 114d57.598

Lily Lake and Redfish Lake Creek Falls

You can enjoy this delightful hike with small children. The distance and elevation gain is attainable and the scenery is splendid. In season, as one might expect, lily pads cover Lily Lake. Flat slabs of granite offer great picnic spots. As a backdrop, less than a mile away, Heyburn Mountain (10,229 feet) rises more than 3,000 feet from the lake. Redfish Lake Creek Falls is less than a 1/4 mile beyond Lily Lake.

An exhilarating 4-mile boat ride across Redfish Lake, a couple of bridges over fast moving water, a small lake covered with lily pads in season, impressive views of Heyburn Mountain and a waterfall to top it off—what more could a child ask for?

Trailhead Directions

Drive south from Stanley 4.2 miles on Highway 75 and turn right on

Lily Lake and Heyburn Mountain.

paved Redfish Lake Road. Follow this road 1.6 miles and turn right again, following signs for the Redfish Lake Lodge. The lodge is on the left in just 0.4 miles. To get to the trailhead, you must take the Redfish shuttle boat across the lake.

The Hike

After exiting the shuttle boat, follow the signs to "trail" and head straight across the campground. At the restroom, turn left and head along the fence to the first opening. Once through the fence the trail crosses swift-flowing Redfish Lake Creek on a well built bridge. After the bridge, another sign on a tree indicates "trail." The trail crosses a small creek and then climbs 80 feet to a signed junction. Turn right and sign in at the trail register. The forest sign indicates that Lily Pond is 1/4 mile but it is actually only 0.1 miles. After 100 feet of gain reach the small but gorgeous Lily Lake.

To reach the falls, head south, or left, around the pond on the well-worn trail. The trail will drop a few feet then make a 100-foot gain and in 0.2 miles reach the falls. Although no more than 25 feet high, the falls are particularly breathtaking in early season.

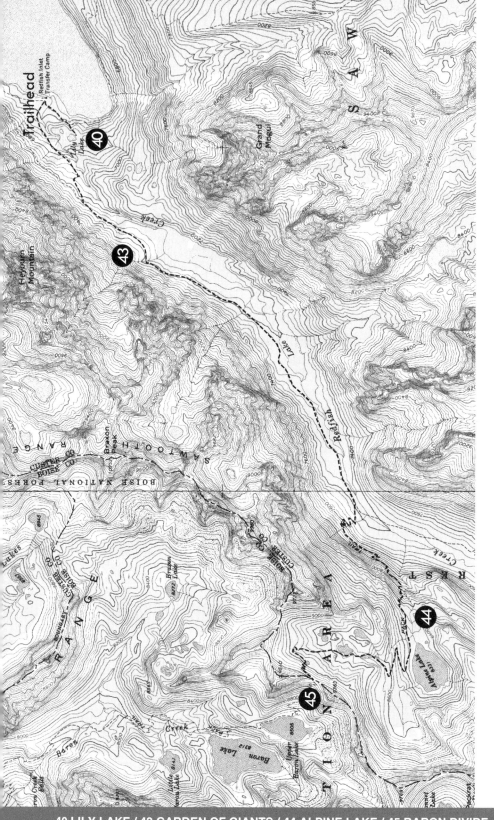

Fishhook Creek Trail

Distance: 5.8 miles roundtrip

Total Elevation Gain: 300 feet

Difficulty: Easy

Elevation Range: 6550 feet to 6850

Topographic Map: Stanley

Time: 2 hours 15 minutes to 3 hours 15 minutes

Distance to trailhead: 5.9 miles

Water Availability: Readily available along Fishhook Creek

Cautionary Advice: *None*

Additional Information: Sawtooth National Recreation Area (208) 774-3000

Coordinates

Trailhead:

North 44d08.906
West 114d55.202

Unnamed creek past Fishhook Meadow:

North 44d08.320
West 114d58.211

Fishhook Creek Trail

For those looking for a relatively flat trail near Redfish Lodge, this is your hike. A well-canopied forest offers nice sun protection. For those with children, translucent Fishhook Creek flows next to the trail so that anytime during the first mile you can create your own turnaround or picnic spot.

The trail leads to the beautiful Fishhook Creek Meadow. From this meadow, spectacular views are offered of Heyburn Mountain (10,229 feet), the imposing Horstmann Peak (10,470 feet) and the distant Mount Ebert (9,882 feet). The trail ends at an unnamed creek that drains an unnamed lake that lies just below Thompson Peak (10,761 feet), the highest peak in the Sawtooth Range. Aspens along the trail make a colorful hike in the fall. The trail gets heavy use up to the meadow.

Trailhead Directions

Drive south from Stanley 4.2 miles on Highway 75 and turn right on paved Redfish Lake Road. Follow this road 1.7 miles and turn right into the large dirt parking lot.

The Hike

From the parking area, follow a small path northwest about 300 feet and cross the paved road leading to the lodge. Across the road is the Redfish Lake trailhead. Note that the Stanley 7.5 quad shows the trail beginning as a dirt road. This is no longer accurate because the entire hike is along a maintained trail.

Leaving the trailhead, the trail gradually gains elevation as it traverses up a sagebrush-covered hillside. After 0.3 miles and a 150 foot gain, arrive at a signed junction. The trail to the left goes over Fishhook Creek on a small bridge and leads to the inlet transfer camp (Hike 42). Continue straight, paralleling Fishhook Creek through lodgepole and Douglas fir forest. At 0.7 miles, come to another signed junction. The trail to the right leads to Marshall Lake (Hike 46). Continue straight.

At 1.2 miles, the trail narrows and swings right as it pulls away from the creek. Continue along the undulating wooded path and emerge at the northeast side of the meadow, 2.1 miles from the trailhead. This makes a wonderful spot for a picnic. Looking across the beaver pond meadow, the views of the surrounding peaks dazzle.

Most people stop at the meadow but the trail beyond is worthy of additional hiking. The trail enters the official Sawtooth Wilderness as it skirts the edge of the meadow and winds through beautiful woods. After another 0.8 miles, the trail dead ends at a creek that drains an unnamed lake just below Thompson Peak.

N

Redfish

Redfish Campground

Heyburn Mtn Campground

Trailhead

Visitor Center

North Shore Picnic Ground

6569

6556

41

34

6700

6599

6600

Launching Ramp

Launching Ramp

Point Campground

6600

FISH LAKE

6547

6800

6600

6800

6740

7200

Creek

6800

7200

33

7200

6800

7200

7400

7400

BOUNDARY

NATIONAL

7000

7600

7400

7200

32

7600

7000

Fishhole

7200

7000

7600

7800

TOOTH

Redfish Inlet to Bench Lakes to Redfish Trailhead

Distance: 7.8 miles. Distance includes the 0.4 miles needed to hike from the Redfish Trailhead to the Redfish boat dock.

Total elevation gain: 1200 feet

Difficulty: Moderate

Elevation Range: 6550 feet to 8750 feet

Topographic Map: Stanley, Mt. Cramer

Time: 3 hours 30 minutes to 4 hours 45 minutes This time does not include the boat ride to the Redfish Inlet.

Distance to trailhead: 5.9 miles

Water Availability: Redfish Inlet, Bench Lakes

Cautionary Advice: *During July and August, horses may be on the trail from the Bench Lakes down to the Redfish Trailhead. Trail usage is heavy on weekends.*

Additional Information: Sawtooth National Recreation Area (208) 774-3000

Coordinates

Trailhead (Redfish Inlet):

North 44d05.798
Wesrt 114d57.465

2nd Bench Lake:

North 44d06.961
West 114d57.195

Redfish Trailhead:

North 44d08.906
West 114d55.199

Redfish Inlet to Bench Lakes to Redfish Trailhead

This fabulous one-way hike uses the boat service out of Redfish Lodge to get to the Redfish Inlet trailhead. The hike crosses and switchbacks up a steep wildflower-adorned hillside. Views of the pristine Redfish Lake and the surrounding peaks that include Heyburn Mountain, the Grand Mogul and Decker Peak, make an outstanding scene. After a 2.4 mile hike, the trail leads into the Sawtooth Wilderness to visit two of the five Bench Lakes. From the lakes, the trail then descends back to the Redfish Trailhead along a moraine and offers marvelous views.

Trailhead Directions

Drive south from Stanley 4.2 miles on Highway 75 and turn right on paved Redfish Lake Road. Follow this road 1.7 miles and turn right into the large dirt parking lot. From the parking area, go west and then turn left on the paved road leading to Redfish Lake Lodge. The marina is located behind the lodge on the north shore of Redfish Lake. For information regarding marina hours and costs see Redfish Lake Lodge in the introduction.

The Hike

After departing from the boat, follow a path through the campground to the restroom. Turn right and arrive at the trailhead and a signed junction. Turn right again towards the Bench Lakes and begin hiking on the backside of the campground.

The trail begins a slow incline and at 0.2 miles enters an open hillside. In midsummer, the hillside has a beautiful display of horsemint, yarrow, and arrowleaf balsamroot. At 0.4 miles, make the first of two switchbacks as the trail climbs above Redfish Lake. Make one last switchback and come to a signed junction at 1.1 miles. Turn right, or northeast, toward Bench Lakes.

The trail stays high above Redfish Lake and slowly gains elevation, going in and out of forest. At 1.7 miles, the trail makes the first of two switchbacks and at 2.1 miles opens to outstanding views of Redfish Lake. At 2.3 miles, crest a small ridge and shortly come to another signed junction.

Turn left here towards the Bench Lakes. The forest sign indicates that the first lake is 0.5 miles but it is actually 0.8 miles. Begin hiking on a level trail fringed by goose whortleberry, which provides food and cover for many animals. At 2.4 miles, pass a registration box and officially enter the Sawtooth Wilderness.

After entering the wilderness, make a switchback and begin skirting an open hillside. At 2.8 miles make another switchback and enter the forest again. Go another 0.1 miles to the first Bench Lake.

To navigate to the second lake, continue on the main trail on the left side of the lake and reach the second Bench Lake after just short of 0.2 miles. Enjoy the views and then retrace your steps 1 mile back to the signed junction.

From the junction, turn left, and follow the trail down the ridge toward the Redfish Trailhead. The descent offers staggering views of glimmering Redfish Lake, the towering Horstmann Peak (10,470 feet), and in the far distance Thompson Peak (10,761 feet) and Williams Peak (10,635 feet). Heyburn Mountain (10,229 feet) stands close behind.

Continue along the ridge top as it drops in elevation. The trail will flatten out at 2.6 miles from the junction to Bench Lakes. At 2.7 miles, cross Fishhook Creek and turn right at the next two junctions. Now descend to the Redfish Trailhead, 7.4 miles from the Redfish Inlet. The parking area is across the paved road.

42 REDFISH INLET TO BENCH LAKES

43 Redfish Inlet to the Garden of Giants and Flatrock Junction

Distance: 7.4 miles roundtrip

Total elevation gain: 850 feet

Difficulty: Moderate

Elevation Range: 6550 feet to 7400 feet

Topographic Map: Mt. Cramer, Warbonnet

Time: 2 hours 45 minutes to 4 hours 15 minutes. Time does not include shuttle boat ride.

Distance to trailhead: 5.9 miles

Water Availability: Redfish Lake, several streams, Redfish Lake Creek

Cautionary Advice: *Bring sun protection for the open hillsides.*

Additional Information: Sawtooth National Recreation Area (208) 774-3000

Coordinates

Trailhead:

North 44d05.985
West 114d57.265

Flatrock Junction:

North 44d04.272
West 115d00.173

Redfish Inlet to the Garden of Giants and Flatrock Junction

This moderate hike provides a fabulous display of scenery. It treks along Redfish Lake Creek canyon with serrated peaks lining both sides of the trail. On the south side of the canyon there is an up-close view of Grand Mogul (9,733 feet). Next up, one of the most dramatic granite faces in Idaho: Elephants Perch. On the north side, the trail skirts just below the majestic Heyburn Mountain (10,229 feet), which actually has two summits, only a couple of feet apart, separated by a deep notch.

The trail passes through a scattering of massive granite boulders, also known as the Garden of Giants, which lies just below Mount Heyburn. This is a wonderful area to explore. The hike ends at Flatrock Junction where Redfish Lake Creek navigates over large flat slabs of granite. A wide array of wildflowers grow on the open hillsides near the junction.

Trailhead Directions

Drive south from Stanley 4.2 miles on Highway 75 and turn right on paved Redfish Lake Road. Follow this road 1.7 miles and turn right into the large dirt parking lot.

To get to the trailhead, utilize the shuttle boat service from the Redfish Lake Lodge. Details are provided under Redfish Lake Lodge in the Introduction.

The Hike

After departing from the boat, follow a path through the campground to the restroom. Turn right and quickly come to the trailhead. Obtain a wilderness permit here and begin the hike.

Enter the official Sawtooth Wilderness and at 0.4 miles, make a switchback on an open hillside. Views below of Redfish Lake improve. At 0.5 miles, arrive at a signed junction with the main trail that leads to the lodge. Continue straight, in and out of trees, across an open hillside with impressive views of the Grand Mogul to the left and the ominous Heyburn Mountain to the right.

At 1.5 miles the trail arrives at the Garden of Giants. No sign indicates the garden, but the enormous boulders dispersed along the trail will let you know you've arrived. This is a nice area to end your hike if you are out with small children.

After passing through the boulder field, the trail crosses two platform bridges over a marshy area at 1.8 miles. Cross two unnamed streams at 2.1 and 2.2 miles; 500 feet beyond the last stream crossing, a superb flat piece of granite along the creek beckons for a snack break. At 2.6 miles, the trail skirts a hillside boulder field.

The final mile of trail wanders through forest along Redfish Lake Creek and finally comes to Flatrock Junction. Here the trail divides with the right arm leading up to Alpine Lake and the Baron Divide (Hikes 44 and 45) and the left arm heading to the Cramer Lakes. Follow the Cramer Lake trail down to Redfish Lake Creek for nice picnic spots.

44   Redfish Inlet to Alpine Lake

Distance: 11.0 miles roundtrip

Total elevation gain: 1800 feet

Difficulty: Difficult

Elevation Range: 6550 feet to 8350 feet

Topographic Map: Mt. Cramer, Warbonnet

Time: 4 hours 30 minutes to 7.0 hours

Distance to trailhead: 5.9 miles

Water Availability: Redfish Inlet, several streams, Redfish Lake Creek, Alpine Lake

Cautionary Advice: *Many sun-exposed hillsides, bring sun protection.*

Additional Information: Sawtooth National Recreation Area (208) 774-3000

Coordinates

Trailhead:

North 44d05.985
West 114d57.265

Alpine Lake:

North 44d03.955
West 115d01.192

Redfish Inlet to Alpine Lake

In addition to the sights of Hike 43, continuing on to Alpine Lake brings a treasure chest of additional visual delights. Just beyond the junction, wildflowers bloom abundantly in the meadow. Hiking beyond the meadow up the granite benches shows off spectacular views of Redfish Lake Creek Canyon and the towering surrounding peaks. The final destination is Alpine Lake, set in a beautiful forest of subalpine firs and lodgepole pines. West of the lake, sprawl the spectacular granite peaks of the Sawtooths.

Trailhead Directions

Drive south from Stanley 4.2 miles on Highway 75 and turn right on paved Redfish Lake Road. Follow this road 1.7 miles and turn right into the large dirt parking lot.

Alpine Lake

The Hike

Follow hike 43 to Flatrock Junction. At the junction, turn right or northwest and begin hiking on an open hillside. Reach the first of six switchbacks as the trail gains 200 feet along the ridge. In season, wildflowers including indian paintbrush, horsemint, monkeyflower, columbine, cinquefoil and pearly everlasting bloom along this ridge.

After completing the last switchback, the trail traverses the ridge and enters forest 4.4 miles from the inlet. Views are exceptional of the canyon below and of the myriad of 10,000-foot-plus surrounding peaks. At the top of the Sawtooth Range are the towering Reward Peak (10,074 feet) and Elk Peak (10,582 feet).

Reward Peak was given its name in 1927 when Arval Anderson, a surveyor for the USGS, found a note that offered the finder a $25 reward for the note's return. The note was dated 1925.

Over the next mile, the trail makes no less than 14 switchbacks as it gains elevation along the granite benches and ridges. This area resembles a fairylike setting as the trail holds tight to granite walls with forest. Views to the Sawtooth Range west of the trail are superlative. At 5.3 miles, the trail finally flattens out and skirts the edge of Alpine Lake at 5.5 miles.

Redfish Inlet to the Baron Divide

Distance: 14.2 miles roundtrip

Total elevation gain: 2800 feet

Difficulty: Very difficult

Elevation Range: 6550 feet to 9150 feet

Topographic Map: Mt. Cramer, Warbonnet

Time: 6 hours 15 minutes to 9 hours 15 minutes

Distance to trailhead: 5.9 miles

Water Availability: Redfish Inlet, several streams, Redfish Lake Creek, Alpine Lake, several small unnamed lakes beyond Alpine Lake

Cautionary Advice: *Due to the elevation gain and distance, this is a very difficult hike. Individuals need to be in excellent physical condition. The hike travels through many open hillsides and exposed areas, bring sun protection. Upper portions of trail may be snow packed until late July or into early August.*

Additional Information: Sawtooth National Recreation Area (208) 774-3000

Coordinates
Trailhead:

North 44d05.985
West 114d57.265

Baron Divide:

North 44d04.501
West 115d01.430

Redfish Inlet to the Baron Divide

Although difficult, the hike to the Baron Divide is a scenic wonderland. Wildflowers, granite benches, formidable peaks, pristine creeks, splendid mountain lakes and breathtaking views are a few highlights. The final destination is the Baron Divide at just over 9,100 feet. This perch offers unforgettable views of the many cliffs, ridges and peaks of the Sawtooths. Upper Baron Lake and Baron Lake shimmer some 600 and 800 feet, respectively, down below the divide. High peaks, including Warbonnet Peak (10,210 feet), Monte Verita (10,102 feet) and Mount Alpen (9,704 feet), are less than two miles away. With so many rock spires and granite peaks, it is easy to recognize why this area is one of the premier rock climbing locations in the Sawtooth Range.

Trail past pond leading to the Baron Divide.

Trailhead Directions

Drive south from Stanley 4.2 miles on Highway 75 and turn right on paved Redfish Lake Road. Follow this road 1.7 miles and turn right into the large dirt parking lot.

The Hike

Follow Hike 43 to Flatrock Junction and Hike 44 to Alpine Lake. Just beyond Alpine Lake, the main trail begins a series of three switchbacks through woods. After a 300 foot climb, the trail levels temporarily before crossing a small stream and then makes a 150 foot climb to the edge of a small unnamed alpine lake at 6.3 miles. In season, a multitude of wildflowers adorn this very scenic setting with a majestic granite spire (9,727 feet) just beyond the lake.

From the small lake, the trail begins climbing again through forest. At 6.6 miles, the trail breaks out into the open and traverses a rocky talus hillside before arriving at a tiny pond. Here, make the first of four switchbacks and arrive at the divide 7.1 miles from the trailhead.

Redfish Trailhead to Marshall Lake

Distance: 9.6 miles roundtrip

Total elevation Gain: 1850 feet

Difficulty: Difficult

Elevation Range: 6550 feet to 8050

Topographic Map: Stanley

Time: 4 1/2 hours to 6 3/4 hours

Distance to trailhead: 5.9 miles

Water Availability: Near the trailhead along Fishhook Creek. After Fishhook Creek no reliable water can be found until you reach Marshall Lake.

Cautionary Advice: *No reliable water once the trail leaves Fishhook Creek until Marshall Lake. The Stanley 7.5 quad map does not show a small portion of the trail, 0.6 miles, that leads from Fishhook Creek to the Alpine Way trail. However, the trail is very well marked. The first 2 miles of trail are exposed and can be hot in summer. Bring sunscreen and a hat. Mosquitoes can be pesky near the lake.*

Additional Information: Sawtooth National Recreation Area (208) 774-3000

Coordinates

Trailhead:

North 44d08.906
West 114d55.202

Marshall Lake:

North 44d09.510
West 114d59.111

Redfish Trailhead to Marshall Lake

Nestled below the towering Williams Peak (10,635 feet), scenic Marshall Lake shimmers. In route to the lake, the trail heads up a hillside and then gains elevation along a wonderful ridge. Divine views of the front range of the Sawtooths are spectacular from here. Superb views of Redfish Lake and Fishhook Meadow can also be seen below. After leaving the ridge, the trail enters the Sawtooth Wilderness and begins a gradual climb through lodgepole and subalpine forest to Marshall Lake. Wildflowers can be found along most of the trail. In early fall the first 2 miles of trail have many aspen, making this hike especially magical.

Trailhead Directions

Drive south from Stanley 4.2 miles on Highway 75 and turn right on paved Redfish Lake Road. Follow this road 1.7 miles and turn right into the large

Marshall Lake

dirt parking lot.

The Hike

From the parking area, follow a small path northwest about 300 feet and cross the paved road leading to the lodge. The Redfish Lake trailhead is across the road. Note that the Stanley 7.5 quad shows the trail as a dirt road. This is no longer accurate because the first part of the trail has since been relocated from the old dirt road.

From the trailhead, the trail gradually gains elevation and leads up a sagebrush-covered hillside. After 0.3 miles and a 150 foot gain, the trail comes to a signed junction. The trail to the left goes over Fishhook Creek on a small bridge and leads to the inlet transfer camp and the Bench Lakes (Hike 42). Continue straight, paralleling Fishhook Creek through lodgepole and Douglas fir forest. At 0.7 miles, come to another junction. The trail straight ahead leads to Fishhook Meadow (Hike 41). At this junction, turn right towards Marshall Lake.

The trail begins a steep climb up a ridge through sagebrush. Lupine and horsemint flourish in season. At 0.9 miles, enter an aspen stand and make the first of two switchbacks. Views of Redfish Lake below improve. Come to a junction at 1.3 miles, 500 feet above Fishhook Creek. The right fork leads to the Alpine Way Trailhead in 2 miles. Turn left or west and begin a gradual ascent along the exposed crest of the ridge. Along the way, several footpaths lead to the top of the ridge and reveal outstanding views of the Sawtooths and the Fishhook Creek drainage. Those with small children will find this location an excellent turnaround spot.

At 2.2 miles, the trail leaves the ridge and then enters the Sawtooth Wilderness at 2.3 miles. After another mile of hiking the trail turns north at 3.7 miles along an open hillside that shoulders Williams Peak. During midsummer, this area has a beautiful display of lupine and arrowleaf balsamroot interspersed with sagebrush. From here, the trail traverses the open hillside and begins to descend to Marshall Lake at 4.2 miles. Reach the first of four switchbacks at 4.3 miles and bottom out at 4.7 miles. The best way to get to Marshall Lake is to continue along the main trail to the outlet stream and turn left or west following a faint trail. The grassy area around the lake can be very marshy in early summer.

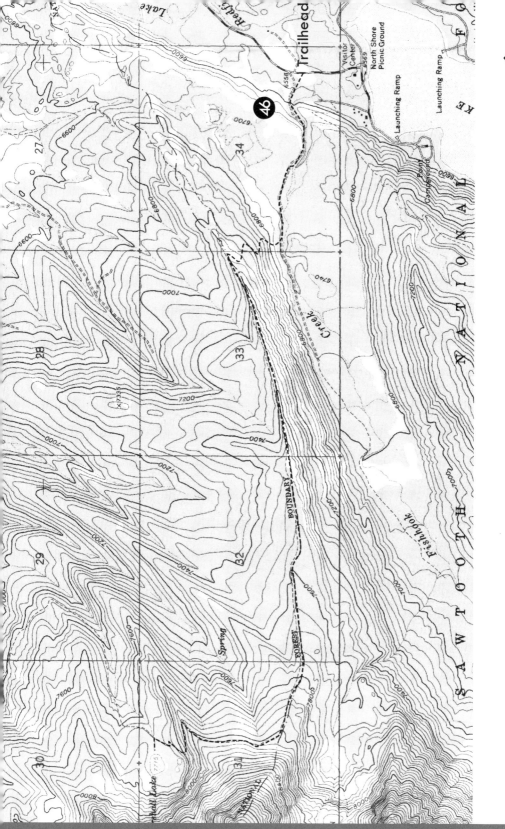

DAY HIKING EQUIPMENT CHECKLIST

- ☐ Hiking Boots
- ☐ Day Pack
- ☐ Trail Map
- ☐ Compass/GPS
- ☐ Water in water bottles
- ☐ Water Filter
- ☐ First Aid Kit
- ☐ Moleskin
- ☐ Flashlight
- ☐ Waterproof matches
- ☐ Food/Snacks

- ☐ Rain Gear
- ☐ Jacket
- ☐ Sunglasses
- ☐ Sunscreen/Lip Balm
- ☐ Insect Repellent
- ☐ Toilet Paper
- ☐ Hat
- ☐ Watch
- ☐ Zip-lock Bags
- ☐ Personal ID
- ☐ Small Pocket Knife

The list is only a suggestion of items

About Scott Marchant

Scott discovered hiking in his early 20's in California. On a vacation to Idaho, he fell in love with the endless wilderness, rugged mountains, and its history. He now calls Idaho home.

During winter, Scott Marchant lives in Boise, Idaho and spends his summers hiking and backpacking in the mountains around Stanley. For the past five years, Scott and his four children have made this wonderful mountain terrain their playground.

In *The Day Hiker's Guide to Stanley, Idaho*, he shares his passion for the area by featuring 46 of his favorite hikes. He hopes that you too will discover this very special place.